Cambridge Elements ☰

Elements in Forensic Linguistics
edited by
Tim Grant
Aston University
Tammy Gales
Hofstra University

AUTHORSHIP ANALYSIS IN CHINESE SOCIAL MEDIA TEXTS

Shaomin Zhang
Guangdong University of Foreign Studies

CAMBRIDGE
UNIVERSITY PRESS

CAMBRIDGE
UNIVERSITY PRESS

Shaftesbury Road, Cambridge CB2 8EA, United Kingdom

One Liberty Plaza, 20th Floor, New York, NY 10006, USA

477 Williamstown Road, Port Melbourne, VIC 3207, Australia

314–321, 3rd Floor, Plot 3, Splendor Forum, Jasola District Centre,
New Delhi – 110025, India

103 Penang Road, #05–06/07, Visioncrest Commercial, Singapore 238467

Cambridge University Press is part of Cambridge University Press & Assessment,
a department of the University of Cambridge.

We share the University's mission to contribute to society through the pursuit of
education, learning and research at the highest international levels of excellence.

www.cambridge.org
Information on this title: www.cambridge.org/9781009494632

DOI: 10.1017/9781009324298

First published 2024

A catalogue record for this publication is available from the British Library.

ISBN 978-1-009-49463-2 Hardback
ISBN 978-1-009-32425-0 Paperback
ISSN 2634-7334 (online)
ISSN 2634-7326 (print)

Authorship Analysis in Chinese Social Media Texts

Elements in Forensic Linguistics

DOI: 10.1017/9781009324298
First published online: March 2024

Shaomin Zhang
Guangdong University of Foreign Studies

Author for correspondence: Shaomin Zhang, 157275000@qq.com

Abstract: This Element explores the sentiment and keyword features in both authorship profiling and authorship attribution in social media texts in the Chinese cultural context. The key findings can be summarised as follows: firstly, sentiment scores and keyword features are distinctive in delineating authors' gender and age. Specifically, female and younger authors tend to be less optimistic and use more personal pronouns and graduations than male and older authors, respectively. Secondly, these distinctive profiling features are also distinctive and significant in authorship attribution. Thirdly, authors' mindsets, shaped by inherent hormonal influences and external social experiences, plays a critical role in authorship. Theoretically, the findings expand authorship features into underexplored domains and substantiate the theory of mindset. Practically, the findings offer some broad quantitative benchmarks for authorship profiling cases in the Chinese cultural context, and perhaps other contexts where authorship profiling analyses have been used. This title is also available as Open Access on Cambridge Core.

Keywords: forensic linguistics, authorship profiling, authorship attribution, sentiment and keyness analysis, Chinese social media texts

ISBNs: 9781009494632 (HB), 9781009324250 (PB), 9781009324298 (OC)
ISSNs: 2634-7334 (online), 2634-7326 (print)

Contents

Series Preface   1

Prologue: The Neglected Language Clue and Recondite
Forensic Linguistic Evidence in a Real 'Suicide Notes' Case   1

1 Introduction   4

2 Research Design   13

3 Results and Discussion   20

4 Conclusion   96

References   99

Series Preface

The Elements in Forensic Linguistics series from Cambridge University Press publishes across four main topic areas: (1) investigative and forensic text analysis; (2) the study of spoken linguistic practices in legal contexts; (3) the linguistic analysis of written legal texts; (4) explorations of the origins, development, and scope of the field in various countries and regions.

Situated in investigative text analysis, Zhang's Element, *Authorship Analysis in Chinese Social Media Texts*, makes several important contributions to the field. First, it provides a rare contribution to the authorship analysis literature in Chinese. Most of the literature in this area is still dominated by English language analyses, and although this situation is now slowly changing, non-English contributions to this field are still to be hugely welcomed. Second, it combines two distinct areas of authorship analysis work: sociolinguistic profiling and attribution. This discussion is particularly valuable, as it demonstrates how stable authorship characteristics associated with extra-textual social or psychological variables can be used to help identify or exclude an individual from an authorship problem. Finally, Zhang introduces and explores the use of sentiment analysis as a form of linguistic profiling to examine how it might be used as part of an authorship analysis. This novelty will make for a much read and cited Element.

This is now the third Element in Forensic Linguistics to focus on issues of authorship; the others are my own contribution, *The Idea of Progress in Forensic Authorship Analysis*, and Andrea Nini's *A Theory of Linguistic Individuality for Authorship Analysis*. Read together, these three Elements represent the history, method, theory, and breadth of work in this area of forensic linguistic research, and we actively encourage further contributions in this area and in the other areas that the series covers.

Tim Grant

Series Editor

Prologue: The Neglected Language Clue and Recondite Forensic Linguistic Evidence in a Real 'Suicide Notes' Case

The *Yangcheng Evening News* reported that on 16 September 2014, a male researcher from Guangzhou University was tragically discovered in his office, having seemingly taken his own life. He was found hanging, his hands tied behind his back. At the scene, police uncovered seven suicide notes, which, the police insinuated, pointed to a clear case of suicide. This led them to end their investigation abruptly.

However, this conclusion that the incident was a 'suicide case' sparked controversy and criticism, particularly from the deceased researcher's family.

They expressed doubts, questioning the plausibility of a scenario where a person could simultaneously hang himself while securing his hands behind his back using a computer cable. Their scepticism, based on the peculiar circumstances surrounding the death, suggested a possibility of foul play, casting doubts on the suicide theory.

Of notable interest, yet seemingly overlooked, was a crucial piece of evidence: the aforementioned seven suicide notes discovered in the deceased researcher's office. This oversight may have been unintentional, perhaps due to the police's lack of awareness of the potential significance that these suicide notes might hold for further forensic linguistic analysis and investigation.

Regardless, the decision to conclude the case without deeper and further scrutiny could only have compounded the trauma already experienced by the family. It was clear that further investigation into these suicide notes could have cast new insights into the case and should not have been dismissed so lightly.

Conducting a further and comprehensive examination of evidence such as the seven suicide notes is obviously an essential and crucial aspect of the ongoing police investigation. Drawing upon the analytical techniques used by forensic linguistics could add to this police work. Using the suicide notes as clues, a forensic linguist could conduct an authorship attribution analysis to decide *who* wrote the suicide notes by collecting and comparing texts confirmed to be the deceased researcher's own personal writings during his lifetime. Through attribution analysis, if the alleged suicide notes align with the researcher's established writing style as evidenced in these baseline texts, an opinion could be formed that he most likely committed suicide. Conversely, if the so-called suicide notes do not match, it necessitates further investigation into possible forgery of the suicide notes and raises questions about potential suspect(s). That analysis would argue for the case to not be prematurely categorised as suicide.

For forensic linguists, authorship attribution serves as an indispensable tool in identifying suspects, although it is not the sole method that can be used in police investigations. Unfortunately, such promising forensic linguistic evidence is still hidden from public view and not yet commonly recognised, especially by law enforcement and the judiciary in China. The invisibility and unrecognisability of such evidence might partly be attributed to the inconsistency and lack of systematisation in authorship analysis research. Other contributing factors could be biased perceptions of the role of linguistic analysis and the absence of clearly defined and relevant regulations concerning forensic linguistic evidence.

As a result, forensic linguistic evidence is variably and inconsistently handled, leading to inconsistencies in its application and interpretation. While speaker identification evidence is generally admissible in both civil and criminal cases and lie detection evidence may be admissible as peripheral evidence in a few civil cases, largely subject to the discretion of judges, authorship attribution analysis, a significant type of evidence comparable to DNA evidence in several UK criminal cases, is often overlooked in the judicial system. China's Civil Procedure Law specifies documentary evidence rules, but this generally refers to raw documents without further linguistic analysis. One area of forensic linguistic analysis, however, that is a more established domain and universally considered admissible as evidence of forgery and fraud in documents, is handwriting analysis.

Therefore, the future of forensic linguistic evidence's acceptance and admissibility depends on consistent and systematic research in forensic linguistics and the future amendments to the Rules of Evidence. This research requires an unwavering commitment to forensic linguistics and ongoing efforts to advance the field in China. This reasoning motivates the investigation of this area and this Element.

China operates mainly under a civil law system, where judges base their decisions primarily on statutes, not precedents, and there are no opportunities for them to 'make' the law. Therefore, the Rules of Evidence play a more crucial role than the precedents in improving the delivery of justice, forming the foundation of court decisions and significantly influencing police investigations by determining what constitutes valuable and worthwhile case clues. However, most statutes are overshadowed by the rapid development of society. With the digitalisation of documents and the increasing reliance on e-signatures or click-to-verify identity checks, traditional handwriting analysis is at risk. Thus, it becomes increasingly imperative to consider incorporating new types of forensic evidence, like authorship analysis, which are independent of handwriting.

In the foreseeable future, we hope to see amendments to the Rules of Evidence that establish more clearly defined and more consistent standards for evidence admissibility and credibility in court. Such standards should reflect some major progress in forensic science, including the 'recognition of contextual bias in analysts, the need for validation studies, and a shift in the logic of providing identification evidence' according to Grant (2022, abstract page). Such progress would guide the use of various forensic evidence and potentially make authorship analysis and similar forensic linguistic methods more acceptable as court evidence. In this way, the case of the 'suicide notes' should have been subjected to more thorough investigation instead of being hastily closed, ensuring justice for the victim's family. 'Improve the delivery of justice through the analysis of language', the motto of Aston Institute for Forensic Linguistics at Aston University, should resonate with all societies striving for justice.

1 Introduction

1.1 Background and Research Aim

Despite being undervalued as shown in the prologue, authorship analysis has emerged as a crucial academic discipline in delivering justice in society, and its global significance continues to escalate. An increasing number of countries, including the United Kingdom, the United States, and Australia, are recognising the significance of authorship analysis and they are paying considerable attention to this issue in order to promote societal fairness (Grant, 2007; Heydon, 2019; Solan & Tiersma, 2004). However, the significance of authorship analysis cannot be overstated, and it deserves further exploration through testing more promising and robust authorship features in diverse linguistic and cultural contexts.

In the realm of authorship analysis, we already have a solid foundation of well-understood and robust linguistic features, including word length and the type token ratio (Biber et al., 2002; Cunningham & Haley, 2020). However, a crucial need is still to explore and test higher-level linguistic features to further enhance and expand our understanding of authorship. Despite the promising potential of the higher-level and advanced linguistic elements, such as sentiment features and keyword features, they have not received substantial attention in authorship analysis. Fortunately, relentless efforts are still being made to explore these innovative elements within the scope of authorship analysis (Martins et al., 2021; Narayanan et al., 2018; Panicheva et al., 2010; Schneider, 2015). The seemingly subjective nature of sentiment features may lead some to view them as unreliable. However, the effectiveness of some emotion markers, a type of pragmatic feature, has been initially validated as effective in authorship attribution (Zhang, 2016; Zhang, 2021).

Hence, this Element aims to delve into the features related to sentiment and keywords in both authorship profiling and authorship attribution within the Chinese cultural context, drawing upon the perspective of mindset. Specifically, a mindset is characterised as a cognitive filter or lens, significantly shaping our perception of the world (Earley et al., 2007; Gupta & Govindarajan, 2002; Sistek-Chandler, 2019). As such, any written work can be seen as a tangible manifestation of our perspectives, attitudes, and emotions about the world, inevitably shaped by our mindsets.

Moreover, considering Mandarin Chinese holds the status of the world's most frequently spoken language, its importance should not be overlooked in the quest for global justice. Chinese authorship analysis warrants greater public recognition and attention as indicated in the suicide note case study example in the prologue.

1.2 Literature Review

This Element divides authorship analysis into two tasks within the broader field of forensic linguistics: authorship profiling and authorship attribution. Authorship profiling focuses on examining language to deduce potential demographic information about the author, such as gender, age, education, occupation, and native dialect/language (Bevendorff et al. 2022), while authorship attribution scrutinises language to identify the text's author (Ainsworth & Juola, 2018). Although authorship attribution and profiling may appear to necessitate different strategies, it is plausible that these two tasks are interrelated and possess overlapping elements, which could potentially be leveraged to uncover detailed information about a suspect author's background via shared linguistic features.

Therefore, the author of the Element is trying to identify the features that could reveal authors' demographic information consistently and distinctively (Grant, 2013) in authorship profiling, such as gender and age ranges. The next step involves testing the effectiveness of these features in the task of authorship attribution, followed by an exploration of potential relationship between linguistic patterns and authors' demographic information. Prior to commencing this work, it is imperative to undertake a comprehensive review of the literature concerning the relationship between authorship attribution, authorship profiling, and the interplay of these aspects with authorship features and mindset.

1.2.1 Authorship Attribution and Authorship Profiling

As mentioned earlier, authorship attribution and profiling are two separate but interconnected tasks. The interconnectedness is evident and has been stressed as 'both tasks are focused on gaining knowledge about the individual who wrote a piece of text' (Deutsch & Paraboni, 2022, p. 2). Specifically, they believe that profiling predictions, such as gauging an author's gender, age, and education level, can assist in narrowing down the pool of potential authors for attribution tasks. Furthermore, some studies have employed profiling-derived features, like gender, place of residence, occupation, and location predictions, as classifiers to detect and identify aggressive tweets in Mexican Spanish (Casavantes et al., 2019; Garrido-Espinosa et al., 2020).

The studies underscore the symbiotic relationship between authorship attribution and profiling within natural language processing (NLP). They propose that because demographic information and linguistic features remain relatively stable and consistent within a group of authors, the knowledge gained from one task can greatly facilitate the successful execution of the other.

1.2.2 Progress in Authorship Analysis

In recent years, there have been considerable advancements in authorship analysis, with notable strides in both methodological diversity and feature evolution (Bevendorff et al., 2020; Bevendorff et al., 2021; Bevendorff et al., 2022; Wiegmann et al., 2019). Firstly, traditional approaches like logistic regression now co-exist with newer approaches such as n-gram and deep learning (Bevendorff et al., 2020). These approaches are often evaluated individually or in combination. Research (Bevendorff et al., 2020) indicates that the highest performance levels are achieved when combining traditional and new approaches. Consequently, these new approaches are not only welcome but necessary, as they can unlock significant potential when paired with traditional methods in authorship analysis. Specifically, by incorporating new techniques and methods, researchers can gain novel insights into the authorship of a document, which might not be achievable using only traditional methods. This can lead to more accurate and reliable authorship analysis, which is essential in pursuing and upholding social justice. Additionally, embracing these new approaches helps to overcome the constraints of traditional methods and stay current with the rapidly evolving landscape of technology and data analysis.

Secondly, the features used in authorship analysis have evolved from basic lexical and syntactical ones to more sophisticated ones, such as personality traits and emotions, which were seemingly first employed in the PAN 2020 task (Bevendorff et al., 2020). Similar to the evolution of methods, exploring and testing sophisticated authorship features is essential because they can considerably augment the potential of simple features in authorship analysis. In particular, the utilisation of diverse types of authorship features will likely enhance the accuracy and effectiveness of authorship analysis, thereby deepening our understanding of authorship.

However, more nuanced features like sentiment features require further exploration. The effectiveness of such features in authorship analysis has not yet been clearly articulated and demonstrated despite their use in the PAN 2020 profiling task. In addition, despite a very optimistic viewpoint on the emotional-related features, including emotion markers, graduation, and sentiment polarity (Torney et al., 2012; Zhang, 2016), these features have not received much attention in authorship analysis. Similarly, keywords derived from keyness analysis have shown unique potential in authorship analysis based on a preliminary unpublished analysis conducted by the author herself in 2019. However, they too have not received much focus. Accordingly, this Element is dedicated to exploring and testing these promising features in authorship profiling and authorship attribution.

1.2.3 Authorship Features, Idiolect, and Mindset

Sentiment Analysis and Sentiment Score

Sentiment analysis is a recently popularised technique in natural language processing capable of deciphering the underlying attitudes, emotions, or opinions expressed within author-generated texts. Essentially, sentiment analysis quantifies subjective language elements such as opinions, emotions, or attitudes related to a topic, person, or entity (Korenek & Šimko, 2014; Roldos, 2020). Pioneering studies (Martins et al., 2021; Narayanan et al., 2018; Panicheva et al., 2010) have found correlations between authorship analysis and the authors' sentiment.

Panicheva et al. (2010) was among the few researchers to discover that each author individually and uniquely expresses their subjective evaluation and appraisal, thereby linking authorship attribution with sentiment polarity classification. Schneider (2015) explored the efficacy of sentiment analysis in authorship attribution, finding that this new stylometric feature underperformed traditional stylometric features, implying a correlation between authorship attribution and sentiment analysis (Martins et al., 2021; Narayanan et al., 2018; Panicheva et al., 2010). Over the past decade, sentiment analysis has been used to profile and identify authorship despite most related studies not focusing on forensic authorship.

Ezaldeen et al. (2022) generated an e-learning recommendation system for individual learners using sentiment analysis of online reviews to extract individual preferences. Martins et al. (2021) demonstrated how to identify authors' emotional profiles from social media texts through sentiment analysis and use these profiles to improve authorship attribution. According to Narayanan et al. (2018, p. 931), 'sentiment analysis is a valuable asset to authorship attribution'.

These studies pioneered authorship analysis utilising sentiment analysis from the perspective of NLP. However, according to Grant (2007), these computational studies were primarily designed to enhance authorship algorithms or classification models rather than exploring and explaining texts and authorship patterns in relation to demographic factors, which is an essential aspect of forensic linguistic studies. In contrast, forensic linguistics emphasises the exploration and explanation in authorship analysis, which aligns with this Element's main focus: authorship, sentiment, and their relationship.

Keyness Analysis and Keyword Features

The keyness approach, generating keywords, is a very promising corpus technique for exploring discourses of various disciplines (Gabrielatos, 2018; Gries, 2021). Data-driven, keyness-based keywords feature prominently in a text for particular reasons. They are identified due to their statistically significant frequency compared to reference texts (Bondi, 2010; Gabrielatos, 2018; Gries, 2021), offering insights into a text's 'aboutness' (Bondi & Scott, 2010) and 'style' (Bondi & Scott, 2010; Scott & Tribble, 2006; Taylor & Marchi, 2018), which are thought to be indicative of an author's demographic characteristics.

Aboutness denotes a text's main concepts, subject matter, and attitudes (Gabrielatos, 2018; Scott & Tribble, 2006; Zhang, 2021), such as the name of the main characters in a play. Style, on the other hand, is characterised by unique textual qualities and an author's 'position and identity' (Bondi, 2010, p. 7) in a text or corpus, such as the use of pronouns and exclamations (Scott & Tribble, 2006). For example, personal pronouns have been identified as gender features in a study of Chinese language use on weblogs (Zhou, 2007). Additionally, intensifiers, which are part of graduations (Martin & White, 2005), should also be considered part of the 'style' of a text as they are gender-related features and could potentially be the clue to distinguishing the gender of a Chinese weblog writer (Zhou, 2007).

Keyness analysis, by generating keywords, provides a robust technique to explore both the similarities (Kilgarriff, 1997; Taylor, 2013) and the differences (Kilgarriff, 1997; Scott, 1998) between texts or corpora because 'any difference in the linguistic character of two corpora will leave its trace in differences between their word frequency lists' (Kilgarriff, 1997, p. 233).

Furthermore, based on preliminary research titled 'From Keywords to Authorship Profiling: A Keyness Approach' (Zhang, 2019) and its findings, the keyness approach demonstrates its effectiveness in identifying clues to various profiling characteristics of a text's author. Statistically, as mentioned earlier, the keyness-based keywords or key phrases are words or phrases with a frequency which is statistically significant (Bondi, 2010; Gabrielatos, 2018; Gries, 2021). Linguistically, these words or phrases make the text distinctive (Gabrielatos, 2018). Therefore, it is hypothesised that the keyness approach could provide clues to an author's identity despite not being specifically designed for authorship profiling.

Furthermore, the keyness approach is noteworthy for two more reasons. Firstly, a pilot exploration has found that this approach is not sensitive to the length of the observed texts, which allows for the exploration of short texts for potential authorship profiling. Even a very brief text could generate a keyword list with the aid of the keyness approach. Secondly, the approach is cross-linguistic, making it possible to analyse the authorship of anonymous texts written in any language, a feature especially useful in investigating transnational crimes.

Authorship Features and Idiolect

An author's idiolect is composed of a habitual and unique combination (McMenamin, 2002) and co-selection of various authorship features. The term 'co-selection' refers to the simultaneous choice or use of multiple linguistic features, much like how a person's shopping habits reflect their specific needs and individual preferences. For instance, the habitual shopping list of a cat owner would significantly differ from that of a parent with a baby. Just as individuals can be differentiated by the unique combinations of items on their shopping lists, which are tailored to their particular circumstances and lifestyle, writers exhibit a 'linguistic shopping list'. This list encompasses their preferred vocabulary, syntactic patterns, and other linguistic styles used consistently and distinctively (Grant, 2013) within their writing. These specific features that make up an individual's 'linguistic shopping list' are not random assortments but are often used together in a patterned way. These patterns, unique and distinct to each person, comprise their linguistic fingerprints, or idiolects, and can be pivotal in distinguishing one individual's language use from another's. This is because, while many people might share some features, the exact pattern of co-selected features is highly individual.

In the context of this Element, whether the patterned combination of the aforementioned authorship features can constitute distinct and unique aspects of authors' idiolects is assessed. Each idiolect is considered a distinct pattern of linguistic features. Consequently, subsequent sections use the term 'pattern' in this specific sense, denoting the individualised linguistic characteristics that comprise a person's idiolect.

Authorship Features and Mindset

An author's unique set of linguistic features constitutes their idiolect, reflecting individual choices in language use. This idiolect is not just a set of random linguistic features; it is closely tied to the author's mindset, mirroring cognitive patterns, and perspectives. Therefore, there exists a profound interconnection between our linguistic preferences and our mental frameworks.

As noted earlier, a mindset is defined as a cognitive filter through which we look at the world (Earley et al., 2007; Gupta & Govindarajan, 2002; Sistek-Chandler, 2019). Thus, our mindset, encompassing our beliefs, values, attitudes, and perspectives, influences our decision-making processes, habitual ways of thinking, and communication styles (Pourdehnad et al., 2006; Sistek-Chandler, 2019). This, in turn, affects the words we select and how we express ourselves. Consequently, the writings are essentially filtered through the author's mindset.

Synchronically, these writings combine various linguistic features. Some of these features remain consistent across an author's body of writings and distinctive enough to differentiate one author from another (Grant, 2013). Such features in combination form what could be referred to as the author's writing patterns or habits, which are important for characterising and predicting authorship. It is believed that such writing habits or patterns develop as a result of an action-oriented mindset which is characterised by a focus on taking action and getting things done quickly (Verplanken & Orbell, 2019). This contrasts with a deliberative mindset that focuses on careful consideration and analysis prior to taking action (Verplanken & Orbell, 2019). While these two mindsets may seem contradictory, they generally co-exist in each individual and can actually complement each other in certain circumstances.

Diachronically, our mindsets are relatively stable, given that 'our mindsets are a product of our histories' (Gupta & Govindarajan, 2002, p. 116). They remain relatively stable and consistent because they are embedded within people's attitude and belief system. This differs from a stance which is more situational and can change from topic to topic. Therefore, under the influence of our mindsets, our writing habits or patterns can be sticky and hard to change because 'even if one chooses to act differently, a habit may easily take over' (Verplanken & Orbell, 2019, p. 76). However, the relative stability of a mindset does not imply stagnation. Our mindsets also 'evolve through an iterative process' (Gupta & Govindarajan, 2002, p. 116). Consequently, our linguistic features should also be relatively stable but capable of gradual evolution.

This Element adopts mindset as its central perspective due to its role as a specific way of thinking, characterised by a psychological predisposition to certain thought patterns and behaviours. This unique cognitive framework is hypothesised to serve as the psychological bedrock underlying an individual's implicit thought processes and explicit linguistic patterns or idiolect.

Idiolect and Mindset

A person's idiolect is a linguistic manifestation of their mindset, which is postulated to underlie and drive these unique linguistic patterns. Since mindset refers to the established set of attitudes held by someone, it is a predisposition to think or feel in a certain way. The way individuals express themselves through their idiolect can reflect their mindset. For instance, an optimistic person may use certain phrases, expressions, or types of syntax that convey positivity, which would be evident in their idiolect. Conversely, a pessimistic or critical mindset might influence a person to use more negative language or critical phrasings. Mindset influences perception and thought patterns, which in turn affect communication and language use. Someone with a growth mindset, who believes they can improve with effort, might use language that is more open, hopeful, or focused on progress and learning. In contrast, someone with a fixed mindset might use more absolute or limiting language.

Idiolects can also provide social cues about a person's mindset. For instance, the consistent use of certain phrases or styles of speaking can signal a mindset even if it's not explicitly stated. In addition, the relationship is dynamic, meaning changes in a person's mindset over time might reflect changes in their idiolect as well.

In linguistic studies, analysing idiolects can provide insights into a person's mindset, though it's a complex endeavor requiring consideration of various factors beyond just the words used. In psychology and sociolinguistics, understanding this relationship might involve looking at how language use both influences and is influenced by cognitive processes, social identity, group memberships, and personal aspirations.

In summary, while idiolects are a manifestation of individual linguistic choices and styles, they are influenced by and reflective of a person's mindset, though this relationship is multifaceted and influenced by several external and internal factors. This interplay can be a rich area of study, particularly in fields interested in the intersections of language, psychology, and social identity. The exploration of the interplay between authors' patterned idiolects and mindset is a key aspiration of this Element.

Mindset, Gender, and Age

The impact of mindset on both gender and age has been explored as well. Several sociocultural studies (Degol et al., 2018; Lee et al., 2021; Sistek-Chandler, 2019) have highlighted a trend where, in certain contexts, females are often less motivated than males in academic or career pursuits, partly due to a prevailing gender-stereotyped mindset. These studies suggest that challenging and transforming such a stereotyped mindset could be instrumental in fostering an environment that encourages and enhances females' achievements. Some biological studies have found correlations between sex hormones, neural structures, and differences in emotional expression between males and females (Berenbaum & Beltz, 2016; Einstein et al., 2013; Pennebaker, 2011a; Pennebaker, 2011b). An experiment involving transgender men who had undergone successful hormone treatment showed changes in their ways of emotion processing (Kiyar et al., 2022).

Besides, some research suggests that women experience and report more negative emotions because they are capable of perceiving and responding more intensely to unpleasant events than men do (Berenbaum & Beltz, 2016; Bianchin & Angrilli, 2012; Fiorentini, 2013; Kring & Gordon, 1998; Latu et al., 2013; Ruberg & Steenbergh, 2011), making them more susceptible and vulnerable to depression.

Lastly, age-related differences in language use may also be influenced by hormones (Shakouri et al., 2015). However, this aspect has received considerably less attention than gender differences.

1.3 Research Questions

Based on the reviewed literature and the research aim, three specific research questions have been formulated as follows:

Firstly, are there significant differences in sentiment scores and keyword features (personal pronouns, exclamations, and graduations) with respect to authors' gender, age, and text genre (authorship profiling)?

Specifically, to investigate the first research question further, three sub-questions have been developed:

1) Are sentiment scores consistent within individual authors?
2) Are sentiment scores distinctive between authors concerning gender, age, and text genre?
3) Are keyword features distinctive between authors in terms of gender and age?

Secondly, are sentiment scores and keywords distinctive features in authorship attribution?

Thirdly, how are the tested distinctive features related to authorship in terms of mindset?

For the third research question, based on the distinctive features of authorship, the related habitual language usage leading to distinctive authorship is explored to detect and confirm the underlying patterns between authorship and mindset.

To answer these research questions, social media texts have been collected. Social media texts are the most complex and intricate forms of language output in China, with various social media platforms serving as spaces for representation, interaction, opinion, and emotions (Kavada, 2015; Neogi et al., 2021). Specifically, three consecutive analyses are conducted to highlight the new features testing and the close connection between mindset and authorship. Firstly, authorship profiling tests based on sentiment and keyness analyses are conducted. Sentiment analysis is used to verify the profiling power of sentiment scores. Keyness analysis is conducted by comparing the social media texts (target corpus) with Texts of Recent Chinese (an established Chinese reference corpus) to detect distinctive authorship clues. Secondly, based on the results of the authorship profiling tests, authorship attribution tests are conducted to gauge the attribution power of the sentiment and keyword features. Finally, underlying connections and patterns between authorship and our mindsets are explored based on the results and the related literature.

By exploring these questions, hopefully, this Element will make three primary contributions to authorship analysis. Firstly, it aims to deepen our understanding of how sentiment and keywords relate to authorship. Secondly, it seeks to enrich both the theory and practice of authorship analysis by elucidating the intriguing relationship between authorship features, authors' demographic information, and our mindsets. Thirdly, it is also hoped that this Element will heighten public awareness about the significance of Chinese authorship analysis in pursuing social justice both domestically and globally.

2 Research Design

2.1 Methods and Tools

A snowball sampling method was adopted to assess the sentiment-related and keywords-related linguistic features for authorship profiling and authorship attribution in the Chinese language context from the perspective of mindset. This allowed for collecting reliable written texts on social media from known authors. A mixed-method approach was also employed, primarily incorporating sentiment analysis and keyness analysis to scrutinise the texts.

Specifically, sentiment analysis, which could identify the emotional tone behind a body of texts (Paschen, 2020), was chosen to measure the sentiment of the texts believed to be associated with authorship (Martins et al., 2021; Narayanan et al., 2018; Panicheva et al., 2010; Schneider, 2015). Keyness analysis, a very promising corpus linguistic approach to exploring discourse (Gabrielatos, 2018; Gries, 2021), was employed to identify the significant concepts and attitudes (Gabrielatos, 2018; Zhang, 2021) in texts, thereby measuring the similarities and differences among corpora (Kilgarriff, 1997).

The tools used in the study included a sentiment analysis tool to generate sentiment scores, a keyness analysis tool to generate keyword features, and a lexico-syntactic analysis tool to generate lexico-syntactic features with which the performance of the keyword features in authorship attribution could be compared.

Sentiment Analysis and Pysenti 0.1.7

The sentiment analysis was conducted using Pysenti version 0.1.7, a Python-based tool, which was employed to calculate sentiment scores from the collected texts. Pysenti 0.1.7 is a Chinese Sentiment Classification Tool released on 6 April 2021. The tool assigns specific scores to the analysed texts, and these scores are indicative of the authors' sentiments, ranging from pessimistic and neutral to optimistic, thereby offering insights into the emotional tone of the writing. Sentiment scores were computed using models comprising 54,885 sentence structures and dictionaries of weighted sentiment words, adverbs, conjunctions, and denials.

Keyness Analysis and AntConc 4.1.2

AntConc version 4.1.2 was employed to generate keywords for the texts based on the keyness analysis. AntConc 4.1.2 is the most recent version of a corpus tool that incorporates various statistical measures to calculate keyness.

In the keyness analysis, there must be a reference corpus with which the target texts can be compared. A reference corpus, "Texts of Recent Chinese 2019" (ToRCH2019), was used as the reference corpus to compare with the target texts. ToRCH2019 is a ready-made balanced corpus that covers various genres and topics ranging from press to fiction, offering a full-scale reflection of contemporary Chinese. It was originally built in 2014 and was renewed in 2019. The corpus consists of 1,660,038 Chinese characters, 1,008,709 tokenised words, and 61,174 word types in 500 files.

Specifically, by comparing each text with the reference corpus, a keyword list based on keyness was generated. Analysing these keywords provided some linguistic clues to the demographic background. In the subsequent profiling experiments, only the top 10 keywords (selected based on the four-term Log-Likelihood keyness measure and $p < .05$ with Bonferroni correction) of each author's texts were included for analysis to examine related features such as personal pronouns, exclamations, and graduations. Thus, all keywords under consideration were significantly prominent, rendering their presence or absence more consequential than their frequency of use.

Consequently, a binary logistic regression analysis was then applied to investigate the predictive power of the keyword features in determining the gender and age of the text authors. Additionally, the predictive power of both gender and age on the usage of the keywords was also assessed. The results established a reverse causality between the keywords and the demographic background information, namely age and gender, indicating a strong correlation between them.

Lexico-Syntactic Features and WordSmith Tools 8.0

WordSmith Tools 8.0 was used to generate lexical and syntactic features, including measures of word length, type-token ratio, sentence length, and n-gram. These established lexico-syntactic authorship features, frequently used in studies, were compiled and incorporated into a reference feature set. This set served as a benchmark against which the sentiment and keyword features were compared.

Specifically, n-gram features were based on Chinese characters, where an n-gram was a sequence of n-Chinese characters that occur together as a meaningful Chinese word. In the present study, only one- to four-character n-grams were chosen as features in the subsequent authorship attribution tests. This was mainly attributed to the characteristic structure of Chinese words (Zang et al., 2018). The detailed reasons for this selection are elaborated on in Section 3.2.1.

2.2 Data Collection

A snowball sampling method was adopted to collect reliable texts from known authors. This method was chosen over random sampling due to concerns regarding the reliability of texts and the validity of authors' demographic information. The process began with students and friends in my social network, who were invited to refer others from their circles who might be eligible for the research. This process continued until the desired sample size of 115 author texts was achieved. The sample consisted of three types of texts from authors of both genders and from different generations, namely, the older and the younger generations. The sample was balanced in terms of the age groups and gender of the authors.

The age distribution within the sample consisted of 63 younger authors (born around or after the year 2000) and 52 older authors (born around or before the year 1980). This categorisation was based on preliminary sentiment analysis results which showed significant differences between these two groups, namely, the 1980s and the 2000s.

In terms of gender, the sample consisted of 69 females and 46 males. The disparity might have resulted from the nature of my social network. Table 1 provides detailed information about the collected texts and the text authors.

In terms of text types or genres, they were only roughly categorised and controlled. Three types of Chinese social media texts were collected. Type I social media texts encompassed relatively private monologues like Diaries, Blogs, and WeChat Moments. The Diaries and Blogs categories incorporated texts from a diverse array of social media sources, including QQ, Weibo, and

Table 1 Texts and text authors

Diaries, Blogs, WeChat Moments 220,182 Chinese Characters				Online Chats 895,508 Chinese Characters				WeChat Article 21,291,801 Chinese Characters			
Female		Male		Female		Male		Female		Male	
Young	Old	Young	Old	Young	Old	Young	Old	Young	Old	Young	Old
18	5	6	6	18	12	7	10	8	8	6	11

other lesser-known platforms. These were also personal spaces for emotion, grief, and stress. Thus, these texts, generally accessible only to close friends, were assumed to be more emotionally revealing.

Type II texts comprised private dialogues which included Online Chats and instant messaging conversations. The conversations primarily involved two participants. Only two texts were included from single-gender chat groups consisting of more than three people. These texts were assumed to mirror real daily conversations and reveal speaking habits, emotions, and attitudes.

Type III texts consisted of public monologues including articles from WeChat subscription accounts, which were accessible to the public. The authors of these accounts typically express some unequivocal views and attitudes on various issues and topics in these articles. Readers who appreciate an article can "like" it, share it with friends, or even leave a tip for the author. Additionally, readers can subscribe to the author's profile for easy access to their articles in the future. Although these articles were not anticipated to be as emotionally revealing as the type I texts, they tended to reveal authors' attitudes, beliefs, and values.

The three types of social media texts each had unique characteristics. However, these characteristics were not mutually exclusive. For example, type I texts might also reveal attitudes, beliefs, and values, although not as prominently as most type III texts. The distinction lay in the degree of prominence.

There was an imbalance among the three types of texts, mainly due to the limited availability and accessibility of private texts such as Diaries, Blogs, WeChat Moments, and Online Chats. Unlike published works, private texts are not intended for public consumption, and their authors may be reluctant to widely disseminate them. Moreover, private texts are seldom archived or preserved, which makes long-term access challenging.

Initially, the author's education level was also considered as a social factor in text collecting. However, it was not possible to establish diverse educational groups due to limitations in the snowball sampling method and lack of non-higher-education-degree holders among public type III text authors. Only ten were enrolled, which included students from middle and high schools. Besides, among the authors of public type III texts, namely WeChat articles, there existed no individuals without a higher education background. As a result, only one comparative test between university education authors and non-university education authors in the private text was performed.

Specifically, for the purpose of validating the consistency and accuracy of sentiment flow within the longitudinal textual analyses, four text authors were selected for interviews regarding their life experiences during the periods covered by their respective texts. The criteria for selecting these individuals were based on a level of intimacy and familiarity, essential factors in ensuring the authenticity and truthfulness of the information provided during the interviews.

In addition, it is important to note that not all texts from the sampled authors were utilised in every test. The data collection process spanned multiple periods, resulting in a staggered accumulation of data. Consequently, some texts were acquired later than others, affecting their inclusion in certain tests.

Data Management Protocol

Informed consent and anonymisation. During the data collection process, any authors willing to provide their social media writings were informed of the intended purpose of the academic research. This ensured that they understood why both their social media texts and basic personal demographic information were being collected. Personal information was kept confidential to ensure their anonymity, with only the necessary and fundamental demographic details related to their authorship being disclosed.

Public data collection. Some public WeChat account articles were also collected. These articles, being publicly available without password protection, constitute public data and did not require informed consent from the authors for their use (Townsend & Wallace, 2016). They were accessible with a simple subscription click. These included articles written by well-known authors with readily documented demographic information and those by less well-known authors whose demographic information could be easily accessed. Thus, informed consent for using the articles was not required.

Secure storage and separation of demographic and writing data. The collected data were stored on an encrypted server to protect against unauthorised access. Furthermore, the data were also backed up regularly to multiple locations to prevent data loss. In addition, the data intended for analysis, consisting of plain text files without any authors' demographic information, were stored separately. This measure also ensured the anonymity of the data and protected the identities of the text authors.

Aggregate data reporting and avoiding direct quotations. When reporting findings, aggregate data were used to prevent the identification of individual authors. Besides, direct quotations from the texts were deliberately avoided to ensure they could not be traced back to any authors.

Author positioning. The research data also incorporated social media texts written by myself, my friends, and family members, all obtained through informed consent. This inclusion did not undermine the objectivity or validity of the research. On the contrary, familiarity with the authors and their texts potentially enriched the research by allowing me to gain a deeper insight into the correlation between the texts and their authorship. In other words, being acquainted with both the authors and their texts could enable me to understand more profoundly how an author's background, experiences, and worldview might be reflected in their writing. Most importantly, as a researcher, I maintained a steadfast commitment to remain unbiased and objective throughout the research process.

2.3 Data Analysis Process

To address the three research questions methodically, the data analysis process (Figure 1) was divided into three consecutive stages:

Stage 1 focused on testing sentiment and keyword features in authorship profiling, as outlined in Research Question 1. In particular, in this stage, three experiments corresponding to the three sub-questions of Research Question 1 were complemented based on the sentiment and keyness analyses.

Stage 2 was designed to further test the effectiveness of the sentiment and keyword features in authorship attribution. This stage explored whether the

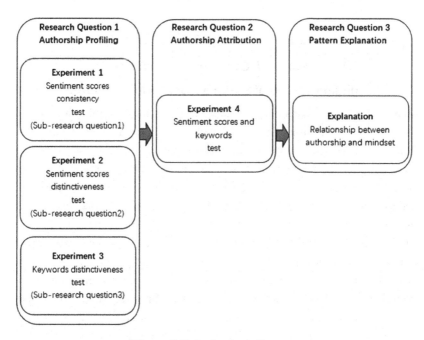

Figure 1 Data Analysis Process

tasks of authorship profiling and authorship attribution could share common features, a concept central to Experiment 4 and Research Question 2. In this stage, sentiment and keyword features were combined into a single feature set and compared against well-established lexico-syntactic authorship attribution features (Biber et al., 2002; Cunningham & Haley, 2020) to assess their performance.

Stage 3 targeted the patterns and connections between authorship and mindset in light of the findings from the first two research questions and related literature, which related to Research Question 3.

Following this process, the results of the experiments were reported, and the established patterns were identified and explained in the subsequent section.

3 Results and Discussion

This section presents and discusses the results obtained from addressing the three research questions in Sections 3.1, 3.2, and 3.3, respectively. Section 3.1 addresses testing of the sentiment and keyword features in authorship profiling through the three designed experiments. Section 3.2 centres on testing sentiment and keyword features in authorship attribution via a fourth designed experiment. Lastly, Section 3.3 focuses on establishing patterns and elucidating relationships.

3.1 Research Question 1: Authorship Profiling

3.1.1 Experiment 1: Consistency of Sentiment Score

Longitudinal Study of Sentiment Scores in Four Authors

Grant (2013) and French and Harrison (2007), emphasised the importance and essence of within-author consistency and between-author distinctiveness of observable features in authorship or speaker comparison. Consequently, as sentiment features are a relatively recent addition to authorship features, the profiling analysis commenced with a longitudinal testing of the consistency of sentiment scores in four authors' texts. This testing aimed to scrutinise their scores closely. The four authors were selected for two primary reasons. Firstly, their offered texts cover a significant period, providing valuable insight into historical events or changes. This is necessary and essential for testing the within-author consistency of a feature across varied timeframes. Secondly, the four authors were both available and willing to discuss some personal experiences, aiding the scrutiny of significant changes in their sentiment scores.

Specifically, the selected four authors comprise two younger females, one older female, and one older male. The two younger females' texts belong to type I data, encompassing Diaries, Blogs, and WeChat Moments. The texts from the older female author and the old male author form part of type II data, primarily Online Chats and instant messaging.

The two younger authors' texts were initially segmented based on their different education stages. These segments were further divided into smaller units, providing sufficient details for scrutinising the consistency of sentiment scores across different stages. The two older authors' texts were initially segmented by year and broken down into smaller units. The texts written by the same author at different stages or in different years were treated as independent groups. This process aimed to test the stability of sentiment scores across various timeframes and years, rather than testing sentiment scores among independent individuals.

1) Sentiment score consistency in the texts of Author 1: a younger female
Overall, the ANOVA test showed a significant difference among the sentiment scores at the $p < .05$ level across the three different stages of education [$F(2, 90) = 4.07, p = 0.02$].

However, the sentiment scores remained relatively stable and consistent during the high school and college stages. Specifically, the post hoc comparisons using the Least Significant Difference (LSD) test revealed that, firstly, there was no significant difference between the mean sentiment scores of the texts written in high school ($M = 41.68, SD = 165.86$) and those written in college ($M = 37.06, SD = 128.30$). In other words, the sentiment scores remained relatively stable and consistent in the first two educational stages from 2014 to 25 June 2019, namely, high school and college. Secondly, the mean sentiment scores varied significantly from college to the postgraduate stage ($M = 138.53, SD = 97.24$) from 8 November 2019 to 10 September 2020. The results are displayed in Figure 2.

Further scrutiny of this tumultuous postgraduate stage was undertaken by examining the stability of the sentiment scores within this particular stage. Therefore, the scores of this stage were further divided into three groups for comparison. The ANOVA test demonstrated that there was no significant difference among the scores at the $p < .05$ level among the three groups [$F(2, 16) = 0.44, p = 0.65$]. Specifically, the post hoc comparisons using the LSD test revealed no significant difference between the sentiment scores of any two groups ($M = 114.91, SD = 88.14; M = 133.20, SD = 133.72; M = 168.37, SD = 94.74$). Therefore, it was reasonable to conclude that the sentiment scores within this upheaval postgraduate stage were consistent.

Forensic Linguistics

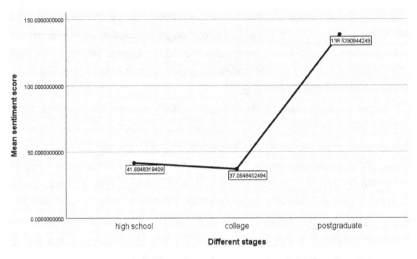

Figure 2 Stability of sentiment scores of Author 1

Until now, both stability and fluctuation of sentiment scores have been observed among the different stages. Whether this could be termed 'relative consistency' (Grant, 2013) is still uncertain. A clearer picture may emerge if compared to an established and relatively stable feature. Hence, average sentence length was chosen as the reference feature as it is well recognised as a 'relevant authorship attribute' (Lehtonen, 2015, p. 817; Rangel et al., 2014; Rangel et al., 2015; Zangerle et al., 2020)

In particular, the same segments of Author 1's texts that were used to calculate sentiment scores were also used to determine the average sentence lengths and to conduct the ANOVA test for stability. Overall, the ANOVA test revealed no significant difference among the average sentence lengths at the $p < .05$ level across the three different educational stages of Author 1 [$F(2, 90) =$ 2.86, $p = 0.06$].

However, the average sentence lengths fluctuated significantly between high school and college. Specifically, the post hoc comparisons using the LSD test revealed a significant difference between the mean average sentence length of texts written in high school ($M = 32.60$, $SD = 18.09$) and those in college ($M = 25.98$, $SD = 9.53$) from 2014 to 25 June 2019. However, the mean average sentence length did not vary significantly when transitioning from college to the postgraduate stage ($M = 25.00$, $SD = 10.71$). Thus, the average sentence lengths were relatively stable and consistent in the final two educational stages from 8 November 2019 to 10 September 2020. Therefore, alongside relative stability, fluctuations existed in the average sentence lengths of Author 1 throughout the three stages. The results are displayed in Figure 3.

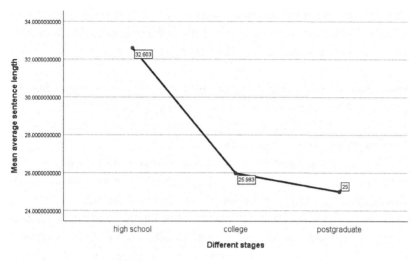

Figure 3 Stability of sentence length of Author 1

Given the relatively consistent performance of the average sentence length, which comprises both stable and fluctuant stages, it appears that the 'relative consistency' (Grant, 2013, p. 480) of the sentiment score in Author 1's texts could be roughly established.

A Closer Examination of the Different Stages of Author 1

Author 1 demonstrated much lower but stable sentiment scores (ranging from 37 to 42) during high school and college (2014–2019), and much higher sentiment scores (139) during her postgraduate period (2019–2022). After a thorough interview and detailed exploration of her longitudinal texts, it was found that she was highly sentimental during her high school years, evidenced by numerous sentimental words, critical ideas, and doubts in her texts during this period. She expressed feelings of confusion and interest in profound topics and frequently discussed her fantasies. Additionally, she expressed dissatisfaction with both her high school and the university she subsequently attended, particularly after her peers entered more prestigious institutions. This dissatisfaction spurred her determination to pursue a master's degree at a more prestigious university, a goal she eventually achieved. This accomplishment likely explains why her sentiment scores surged (139), and she became optimistic during her postgraduate years. During those years, her writings were filled with excitement, and she was enthusiastic about attending various campus lectures and acquiring new ideas.

It is important to note that a more rigorous 'relative consistency' could only be established with more cases involved. Thus, the longitudinal texts of three more authors were further tested and analysed.

2) Sentiment score consistency in the texts of Author 2: a younger female

Overall, the ANOVA test revealed that there was a significant difference among the sentiment scores at the p <.05 level across the three different stages of education [$F(2, 142) = 7.22, p = 0.001$].

However, the sentiment scores remained relatively stable and consistent during the college and postgraduate stages. Specifically, the post hoc comparisons using the LSD test indicated that, firstly, there was a significant difference between the mean sentiment scores for the texts written during the pre-college stage (encompassing both middle and high school periods) ($M = 162.26, SD = 144.57$), those written during college ($M = 90.00, SD = 117.66$), and the postgraduate stage ($M = 27.03, SD = 246.75$) spanning from 2012 to 2015. Secondly, there was no significant difference between the mean sentiment scores of the texts written in college ($M = 90.00, SD = 117.66$) and those in the postgraduate stage ($M = 27.03, SD = 246.75$). This implies that the sentiment scores were relatively stable and consistent during the second and third educational stages from 2016 to 2022. The results are displayed in Figure 4.

In a similar vein, in order to assess the stability of the sentiment scores within the texts of the single upheaval pre-college stage, the scores were further divided into three groups to conduct the comparison. The ANOVA test showed that there was no significant difference among the scores at the $p < .05$ level across the three groups [$F(2, 53) = 1.057, p = 0.36$]. Specifically, the post hoc comparisons using the LSD test indicated that there was no significant difference between the sentiment scores of any two groups ($M = 167.84, SD = 131.01$; $M = 195.17, SD = 180.85$; $M = 127.61, SD = 116.44$). Therefore, it was reasonable to conclude that the sentiment scores within the upheaval precollege stage were consistent.

The performance of the average sentence length in Author 2's texts was also investigated. Overall, the ANOVA test showed that there was a significant difference among the average sentence lengths at the $p < .05$ level across the three different stages of Author 2's education [$F(2, 141) = 2.86, p < 0.001$].

Specifically, the post hoc comparisons using the LSD test showed that: firstly, there was no significant difference between the mean average sentence length of texts written in the pre-college stage ($M = 73.53, SD = 40.84$) and those in college ($M = 80.35, SD = 49.69$). This indicates that the average

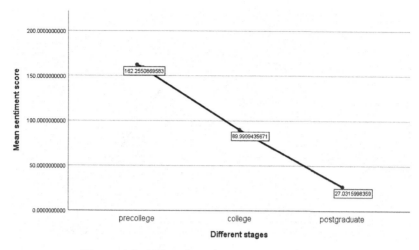

Figure 4 Stability of sentiment scores of Author 2

sentence lengths were relatively stable and consistent in the first two educational stages from 2012 to 2015, namely, middle school, high school, and college. Secondly, there was a significant variation in the mean average sentence lengths when transitioning from college to the postgraduate stage ($M = 23.23$, $SD = 13.17$) from 2016 to 2022. The results are displayed in Figure 5.

A Closer Examination of the Different Stages of Author 2

In contrast to Author 1, Author 2 displayed much higher starting scores (162) in high school (2012–2016). However, the scores steadily decreased (from 90 to 27) during the stages of college and postgraduate studies (2016–2022). Based on the further interview and detailed exploration of her longitudinal texts, it was found that she was very sentimental when she was in high school.

Author 2 was one of the top high school students and she had great expectations for her future. The university she attended was not her first choice but her backup option. Nevertheless, she clarified that this was not the main reason for her decrease in positive emotions. The sudden suicide of a close relative had a profound and devastating impact on her emotional wellbeing. She described the event as the most shocking and distressing of her life. She struggled to move on from the incident, but was unsuccessful.

To make things worse, she contracted tuberculosis (TB) during university and only recovered after a year-long break post-graduation. TB has been found to be closely linked with stress and negative emotions, and could further reinforce

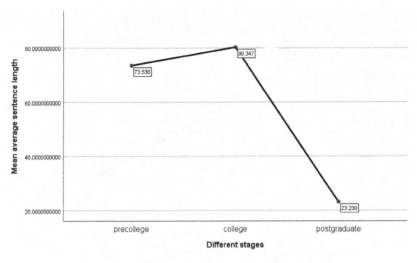

Figure 5 Stability of sentence length of Author 2

these feelings (Nascimento & Bianchi, 2021; Febi et al., 2021). Therefore, it is understandable that her sentiment scores continued to drop.

The following is the demonstration of the sentiment score consistency for the third case: an older female.

3) Sentiment score consistency in the texts of Author 3: an older female

Overall, there was a significant difference among the sentiment scores at the $p < .05$ level across the eight different years of Author 3's texts from November 2015 to October 2022 $[F(7, 369) = 2.65, p = 0.01]$.

However, the sentiment scores of Author 3 remained stable except for two specific years which deviated from the norm. Specifically, the ANOVA post hoc comparisons using the LSD test indicated that: the years 2015 ($M = -30.63$, $SD = 159.61$) and 2017 ($M = 32.67$, $SD = 67.89$) were the two deviations from the main body of the mean sentiment scores of the texts written in the remaining six years. Upon removal of these two years, the ANOVA demonstrated that there was no significant difference among the sentiment scores at the $p < .05$ level across the remaining six different years $[F(5, 300) = 1.96, p = 0.09]$. The results are displayed in Figure 6.

Therefore, it is reasonable to infer that the sentiment scores were relatively consistent and stable across most of the years. The fluctuations occurred only during times of significant emotional turmoil. As Author 3, I can confidently identify the causes of these emotional upheavals in 2015 and 2017 due to their profound impact.

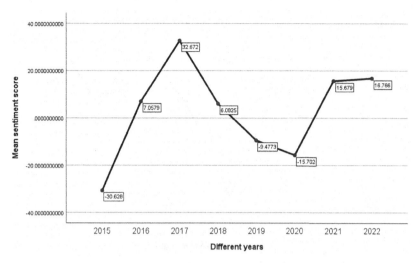

Figure 6 Stability of sentiment scores of Author 3

A Closer Examination of the Years 2015 and 2017 for Author 3

Overall, the year 2015 was very challenging, while 2017 brought promise for Author 3. Specifically, at the very beginning of 2015, I became a full-time university teacher after earning my PhD in forensic linguistics. Unfortunately, frustration ensued when I realised my research interest was not endorsed nor supported as it was not deemed a legitimate discipline. I was even encouraged to change my research focus, leading to my confusion and despair. In addition, I lost one of my cats abruptly in November that year, a trauma that had a lasting impact on my life and strained family relationships. Reflections of such emotional strain were evident in my texts, marking a record low in my emotional history.

However, by the end of 2016, I had transitioned to a different university where I could continue my research. This period marked a record high in my emotional history.

Unfortunately, it was impossible to calculate average sentence lengths from my texts as they consisted of online instant chats. In these chats, sentences were often sent individually without punctuation, closely mirroring spoken dialogue. This phenomenon, where exchanges are made sentence by sentence rather than paragraph by paragraph, is common in online instant chats, rendering punctuation unnecessary.

4) Sentiment score consistency in the texts of Author 4: an older male

For Author 4, overall, there was a significant difference among the sentiment scores at the $p < .05$ level across the seven different years from January 2016 to October 2022 [$F(6, 223) = 2.71$, $p = 0.02$] (Figure 7).

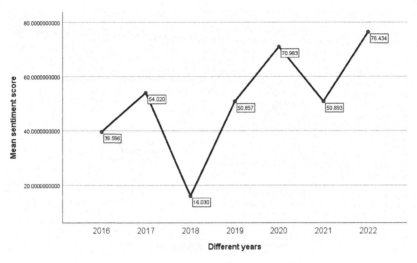

Figure 7 Stability of sentiment scores of Author 4

However, the sentiment scores for Author 4 remained stable except for one specific year where a deviation from the norm was observed. Specifically, the ANOVA post hoc comparisons using the LSD test indicated that the sentiment score for the year 2018 ($M = 16.03$, $SD = 101.81$) was the only outlier which detached from the norm of the mean sentiment scores of the texts written in the other six years. When this year was removed, the ANOVA demonstrated no significant difference among the sentiment scores at the $p < .05$ level across the remaining six years [$F(5, 194) = 1.62$, $p = 0.16$]. The results are displayed in Figure 7.

Therefore, it is reasonable to state that the sentiment scores for Author 4 were relatively consistent and stable in most years, with significant fluctuations arising only amidst intense emotional disruption and turbulence. Based on a subsequent interview with Author 4, it was revealed that a business crisis was the primary cause of the emotional turmoil in 2018.

Author 4's texts were also online instant chats, which precluded the calcula-tion of average sentence lengths.

Summary

In summary, the in-depth analysis of the texts from the four cases supports the argument that the sentiment score is a relatively consistent and stable language feature. The sentiment scores of the four authors showed similar patterns and trends to a well-established consistent feature, namely average sentence length. However, both features demonstrated different patterns across authors, with some exhibiting more consistency and others more variation.

Discussion

Based on the results from the four authors, it is reasonable to believe that the sentiment scores are relatively consistent within authors. However, they are also vulnerable and sensitive to significant emotional changes and disruptions over time. Additionally, the emotional reflections in sentiment scores vary individually. Some authors (Author 1) showed dramatic changes, while others displayed more modest changes (Authors 2, 3, and 4).

Most importantly, the relative consistency of the sentiment scores may be attributed to our mindsets, which are relatively stable as 'our mindsets are a product of our histories and evolve through an iterative process' (Gupta & Govindarajan, 2002, p. 116). Our past histories cannot be overturned overnight, thus, our current mindsets should be relatively stable. Furthermore, our mindset is defined as a cognitive filter through which we view the world (Earley et al., 2007; Gupta & Govindarajan, 2002; Sistek-Chandler, 2019). The filtered outputs, including our emotional and sentiment expressions, should also be relatively stable if this filter is relatively stable.

However, the relative stability of the mindset does not imply stagnation. Our mindsets 'evolve through an iterative process' (Gupta & Govindarajan, 2002, p. 116). Such an iterative evolution process would introduce new changes to the relatively fixed mindsets. Specifically, according to Gupta and Govindarajan (2002), when new experiences and information arise, our mindsets must decide if the new information is consistent with our current mindsets or inconsistent with them. In the former situation, our current mindsets would be reinforced.

In the latter situation, we would experience resistance within ourselves (Lopez, 2020). The final outcome would be either ignoring the new information or changing our current mindsets. Therefore, our sentiment scores vary over time primarily due to the introduction of inconsistent new information and the subsequent changes in mindsets (Gupta & Govindarajan, 2002). Such a change could result in either a positive or a negative emotional shift, which would accordingly cause a rise or fall in sentiment scores. In addition, as each individual has unique life experiences and encounters unique inconsistent new information, each of us has a unique mindset, which results in unique performance and variations in sentiment scores.

In summary, the stability or within-author consistency of sentiment scores was established in the tests presented earlier. Some studies have already used sentiment analysis to predict public mood and conduct opinion mining based on the polarity of emotions (positive or negative) (Albahli, 2022; Birjali et al., 2021; Neogi et al., 2021; Ruz et al., 2022). Martins et al. (2021) even identified authors through polarity of emotions (positive or negative) based on the presence or absence of emotions such as anger, joy, and surprise, along with consideration of authors' categories (politicians and non-politicians). The study treated the combination of these sentiment features as part of an author's writing style even though their main purpose was primarily commercial rather than forensic. However, for the present study, it is premature to assert that sentiment score or sentiment expression is a relevant authorship style until the distinctiveness of the sentiment scores between authors is tested. Therefore, the following sections will focus on testing the distinctiveness of the sentiment scores between authors.

3.1.2 Experiment 2: Distinctiveness of Sentiment Scores

Once the relative consistency of the sentiment scores was established, their distinctiveness (Grant, 2013) was tested in terms of the author's gender, text genre, age, and education, as well as their interaction.

In the following tests, it is important to note that not all sample author texts were used in every test. This discrepancy is because the data were collected over several consecutive periods, and some data were collected at later stages.

1) Distinctiveness of sentiment scores between genders
In this part of the experiment, two separate tests were conducted between female and male authors in private and public texts, respectively. The dichotomy was implemented due to the likelihood of individuals behaving differently when they write or speak privately (e.g., in a diary or small friend group) as opposed to when they do so publicly.

Gender Difference in Private Texts

The section began with a test of the distinctiveness of the sentiment score in private texts, including type I and type II texts for female and male authors.

Specifically, the tested texts comprised 24 texts from female authors ranging in age from about 15 to 72 years old and 16 texts from male authors ranging in age from about 17 to 72 years old. Each author's body of work contained at least one type of text (type I or/and type II). For the 24 female-authored texts, the count of Chinese characters ranged from 4,421 to 13,306, spanning a timeframe from one to 12 years. For the 16 male-authored texts, the Chinese characters ranged from 4,615 to 21,391, spanning a timeframe from one to 13 years.

Overall, there was a noticeable difference in the representation of gender in private texts. Specifically, the standardised sentiment scores revealed that the 16 male texts ($M = 94.02$, $SD = 54.03$), compared to the 24 female texts ($M = 37.08$, $SD = 73.53$), demonstrated significantly higher and more positive sentiment

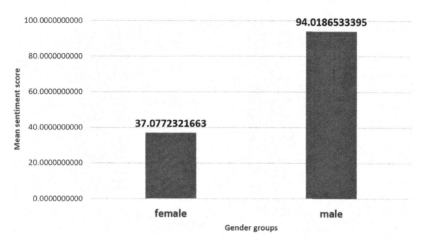

Figure 8 Gender difference in private texts

scores, $t(38) = -2.65$, $p = .012$. The results of the sentiment scores for the females and males in the private texts are presented in Figure 8.

Subsequent to this, there was a test for differences in gender representation in public texts.

Gender Difference in Public Texts

The second test of gender differences focused on assessing the distinctiveness of the sentiment scores in public (type III) texts from both male and female authors. These texts consisted of public articles published on WeChat and available to all subscribers.

Specifically, the tested 15 texts came from female authors aged from 22 to 44 years old and 17 texts from male authors aged from 24 to 52 years old. The 15 female-authored texts contained between 4,318 and 4,361,292 Chinese characters and spanned from four to eight years. The 17 male-authored texts contained between 6,749 and 3,371,270 Chinese characters, spanning from two months to eight years.

Overall, based on the standardised sentiment scores, there was no significant difference between genders in the sentiment scores in public texts, $t(30) = .606$, $p = .549$, although the 17 male texts ($M = 102.16$, $SD = 52.50$) demonstrated slightly lower sentiment scores than the 15 female texts ($M = 114.27$, $SD = 60. 71$). The results of these sentiment scores for the female and male authors in the public texts are shown in Figure 9.

Based on the preceding results, it was observed that the sentiment scores in the female-authored texts varied significantly from 37.08 in private texts to 114.42 in public texts. However, the sentiment scores in the male-authored texts showed only a minor fluctuation from 94.02 in private texts to 101.92 in public

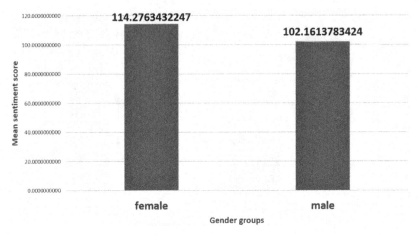

Figure 9 Gender difference in public texts

texts. These variations warrant further investigation into sentiment scores between different text genres within a controlled gender group. As such, the following are the tests of sentiment score distinctiveness with respect to different text genres.

2) Distinctiveness of sentiment scores between different text genres
In this section, two different tests were conducted to compare sentiment scores between different text types, specifically private and public texts, within controlled gender groups.

Genre Difference in Female Authors
The analysis involved 24 private texts and 16 public texts authored by females. Overall, based on the standardised sentiment scores, the 24 private texts ($M = 37.08$, $SD = 73.53$) were compared with the 16 public texts ($M = 114.42$, $SD = 57.76$). The results showed significantly lower and more negative sentiment scores in the private texts written by females, $t(38) = -3.537, p = .001$. The results of the sentiment scores for private and public texts authored by females are demonstrated in Figure 10.

Following this, the difference between the private and public texts authored by males was explored.

Genre Difference in Male Authors
The data set comprised 16 private texts and 16 public texts from male authors. Overall, based on the standardised sentiment scores, the 16 private texts ($M = 94.02$, $SD = 54.03$) were compared with the 16 public texts ($M = 101.92$, $SD = 55.65$).

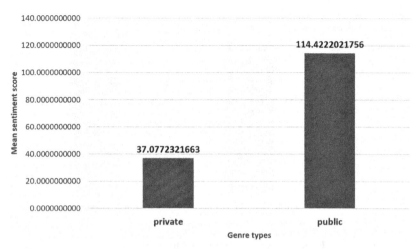

Figure 10 Genre difference in female authors

The results showed no significant difference in sentiment scores across genres of texts authored by males, $t(30) = -.408$, $p = .686$, despite slightly lower sentiment scores in the private texts than the public texts. The results of the sentiment scores for the private and public texts authored by males are demonstrated in Figure 11.

To summarise, the results indicated that the sentiment scores demonstrated distinctiveness between private and public texts only for female authors.

3) Distinctiveness of sentiment scores between different age groups
Similarly, two tests were conducted to compare the sentiment scores between younger and older author groups, specifically those born around 2000 and 1980, in private texts and public texts, respectively.

Age Difference in Private Texts
This section began with testing the distinctiveness of the sentiment scores between different age groups in private type I and type II texts.

The data set included 42 texts from the younger group and 30 texts from the older group. Each author's texts contained at least one type of private text (type I or/and type II). Overall, based on the standardised sentiment scores, there was no significant difference in sentiment scores between different age groups, $t(70) = -1.842$, $p = .070$, despite that the younger group ($M = 55.72$, $SD = 90.51$) showing markedly lower sentiment scores than the older group ($M = 92.10$, $SD = 69.90$). The results of the sentiment scores for the younger and older authors in private texts are shown in Figure 12.

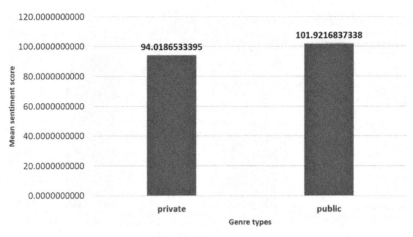

Figure 11 Genre difference in male authors

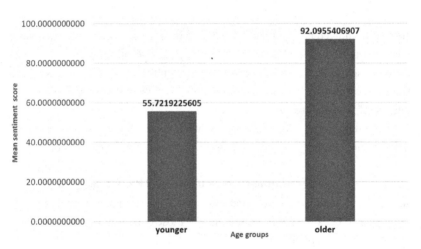

Figure 12 Age difference in private texts

Following this was the test of sentiment scores between younger and older authors in public texts.

Age Difference in Public Texts

The second test focused on the distinctiveness of the sentiment scores across different age groups in public type III texts.

Specifically, the analysis included 14 texts from younger authors and 18 texts from older authors. The results demonstrated that there was no significant difference in sentiment scores between different age groups, $t(30) = 0.608$, $p = .548$, despite the younger group ($M = 114.73$, $SD = 63.76$) displaying

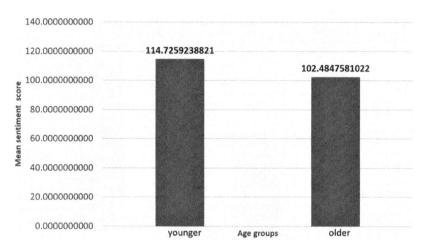

Figure 13 Age difference in public texts

slightly lower sentiment scores than the older group (M = 102.48, SD = 50.20). The results of the sentiment scores for the younger and older authors in public texts are shown in Figure 13.

In summary, based on the preceding results, the sentiment scores of public texts were notably higher than those of private texts for both younger and older groups. A separate exploration of sentiment scores between different text genres was conducted for both younger and older authors to provide a clearer picture,

Genre Difference in Younger Group

This test involved 42 private and 14 public texts written by younger authors. Based on the standardised sentiment scores, the 42 private texts (M = 114.73, SD = 63.76) compared with the 14 public texts (M = 55.72, SD = 90.51) demonstrated significantly lower and more negative sentiment scores, t(54) = – 2.25, p = .028. The results of the sentiment scores for the private and public texts written by younger authors are shown in Figure 14.

Genre difference in older group

Similarly, this test involved 30 private texts and 18 public texts written by older authors. According to the standardised sentiment scores, there was no significant difference in sentiment scores between private texts and public texts in the older group, t(46) = –0.597, p = .554. The 30 private texts (M = 92.10, SD = 69.90) displayed slightly lower sentiment scores than the 18 public texts (M = 102.48, SD = 50.20). The results of the sentiment scores for the private and public texts written by older authors are displayed in Figure 15.

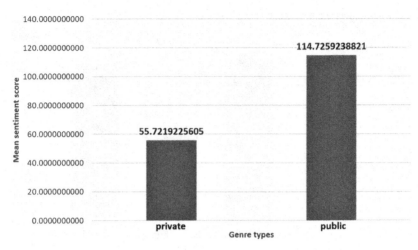

Figure 14 Genre difference in younger group

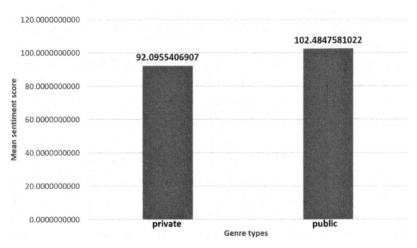

Figure 15 Genre difference in older group

In summary, based on the preceding results, the sentiment scores showed distinctiveness between private and public texts only for younger authors.

4) Distinctiveness of sentiment scores between different education groups
As detailed in the research design, the educational groups could not be fully established due to practical constraints. Thus, in the private texts, only one comparative test was conducted between university-educated and non-university-educated authors.

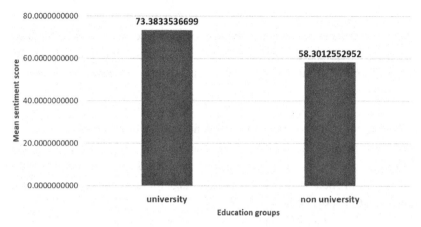

Figure 16 Education difference in private texts

This test included 57 'educated' texts (two extreme outliers were deleted) and 10 'uneducated' texts. Overall, according to the standardised sentiment scores, there was no significant difference in the sentiment scores between the 'educated' and 'uneducated' texts, $t(65) = 0.566$, $p = .573$.

The 57 'educated' private texts ($M = 73.38$, $SD = 81.30$) showed slightly higher sentiment scores than the 10 'uneducated' private texts ($M = 58.30$, $SD = 49.29$). The results of the sentiment scores of the 'educated' and 'uneducated' private texts are displayed in Figure 16.

Summary

In summary, the preceding results reveal significant distinctiveness of the sentiment scores between female and male authors in private texts, and between private and public texts authored by females.

As for the younger and older age groups, even though the distinctiveness of the sentiment score was not statistically significant, the pattern and the interaction between age groups and text genres/types were striking.

Interestingly, a clear trend was observed in both private and public writings. The younger authors ($SD = 90.51$ in private texts and $SD = 63.76$ in public texts) and the female authors ($SD = 73.53$ in private texts and $SD = 60.71$ in public texts) tend to have higher standard deviations in their sentiment scores than the older ($SD = 69.90$ in private texts and $SD = 50.20$ in public texts) and the male ($SD = 54.03$ in private texts and $SD = 52.50$ in public texts) ones, respectively. This result may hint at mood swings or emotional instability in younger and female authors, which will be discussed further later in the study.

However, the sentiment scores were not significantly distinctive between educated and uneducated authors. Moreover, the preceding results highlighted a complex interplay between the distinctiveness of the sentiment scores, gender, age, and text type, suggesting further investigation is needed for a deeper understanding.

5) Testing the distinctiveness of sentiment score in interaction

Based on the preceding tests, this section focuses on exploring the interactions among the distinctiveness of the sentiment scores, gender, age, and text type. More data were collected in this stage for this exploration to ensure representativeness and lack of bias.

Specifically, a factorial three-way ANOVA was conducted to compare the main effects of genre, gender, and age (independent variables) as well as their interaction effects on the sentiment scores (dependent variable). This three-way ANOVA analysis had three levels of genre (Diary Blog Moments, Online Chats, WeChat Article), two levels of gender (female, male), and two levels of age (younger, older). Specifically, in this test, the genre types were investigated in three more-specific categories than the previous ones: the private and public texts. As mentioned earlier, Diary, Blog, Moments, and Online Chats are considered private texts, and WeChat articles are public texts.

The results showed that there was a significant main effect of gender, $F(1, 98) = 4.87, p < .05$, and a significant interaction of gender and genre on the distinctiveness of the sentiment scores, $F(2, 98) = 4.87, p < .05$.

In particular, the main effect of gender [$F(1, 98) = 4.87, p = 0.03$] yielded an effect size of 0.047, indicating that gender accounted for 4.7% of the variance in the sentiment scores. Secondly, the interaction of gender and genre was significant [$F(2, 98) = 3.47, p = 0.035$], indicating a combined effect for gender and genre on the distinctiveness of the sentiment scores. This interaction yielded an effect size of 0.066, indicating that the combined effect of gender and genre explained 6.6% of the variance in the sentiment scores. According to Lakens (2013), $\eta^2 = 0.01$ indicates a small effect, $\eta^2 = 0.06$ a medium effect, and $\eta^2 = 0.14$ a large effect. Therefore, the effect size of 4.7% is nearly a medium effect, and the effect size of 6.6% is a medium effect.

These results suggest that gender and genre contribute significantly to the distinctiveness of the sentiment scores both individually and combined. In order to better understand these results, the corresponding effects of gender and genre in different age groups are illustrated in Figures 17, 18, 19, and 20.

In Figure 17, the younger male authors exhibit higher sentiment scores than the younger female authors in both Online Chats and Diary Blog Moments

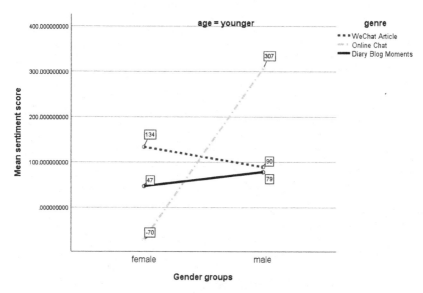

Figure 17 Genre difference in younger females and males

texts, which are private texts. However, when it comes to WeChat articles, namely, the public texts, sentiment scores for male authors are slightly lower, although the difference (134 vs. 90) is not statistically significant. Interestingly, the younger female authors display the highest sentiment scores in these public texts than the younger male ones.

In Figure 18, the older male authors consistently demonstrate higher sentiment scores than their older female counterparts in all three text types. However, the sentiment score difference between the older females and older males (92 vs. 109) in the WeChat articles (i.e., public texts) is not statistically significant, in contrast to the significant gender difference observed in the private texts.

Besides, similar to the case of younger female authors in Figure 17, the older female authors also displayed the highest sentiment scores in the public texts.

Taken together, Figures 17 and 18 reveal two conspicuous patterns in the distinctiveness of the sentiment scores regarding gender and genre: first, male authors generally exhibit higher sentiment scores than female authors. Second, female authors tend to have the highest sentiment scores in public texts compared with private texts.

In addition, Figures 19 and 20 illustrate the distinctiveness of the sentiment scores between different texts, providing a different perspective on the interplay between gender and genre.

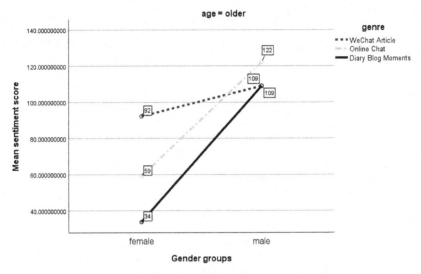

Figure 18 Genre difference in older females and males

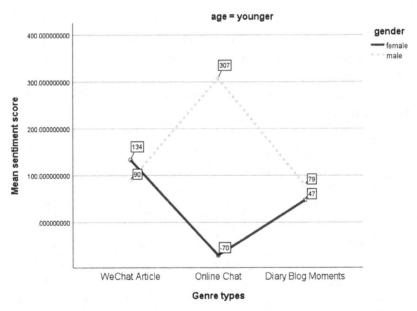

Figure 19 Gender difference in younger authors' three genres

In Figure 19, the younger male and younger female authors exhibit similar sentiment scores in both public WeChat articles (type III texts) and private Diary Blog Moments texts (type I texts). However, significant differences emerge in Online Chat texts: the younger female authors demonstrate notably the lowest sentiment scores across all three text types, whereas the younger

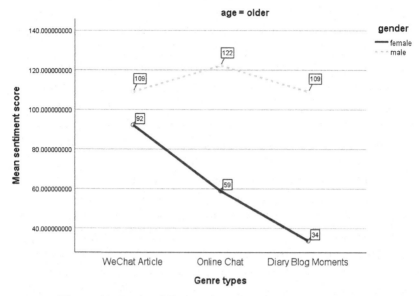

Figure 20 Gender difference in older authors' three genres

male authors display markedly the highest sentiment scores across all three text types.

Figure 20 shows that the older male authors consistently demonstrate higher sentiment scores than the older female authors across all three text types, particularly in the private texts, namely Online Chat texts and Diary Blog Moments texts.

In summary, these four figures present two conspicuous patterns concerning the distinctiveness of the sentiment scores in relation to gender and text type: firstly, female authors display the highest sentiment scores in public texts among the three text types. Secondly, in most instances, male authors exhibit higher sentiment scores than female authors.

Discussion

In the interaction test, both gender and the interaction of gender and genre emerged as significant factors for the distinctiveness of the sentiment scores.

Regarding gender, similar to the pattern in the separate test, the female authors demonstrated statistically significantly lower sentiment scores than the male authors. This suggests that male authors are more optimistic than female authors, a finding consistent with the previous studies (Berenbaum & Beltz, 2016; Bianchin & Angrilli, 2012; Fiorentini, 2013; Kring & Gordon, 1998; Latu et al., 2013; Ruberg & Steenbergh, 2011). Females are thought to experience and report more negative emotions due to their "stronger reactions than men in response to unpleasant events" (Fiorentini, 2013, p. 24; Kring & Gordon, 1998).

As for the interaction of gender and genre, the results revealed that the female authors displayed significantly lower sentiment scores in private texts than in public ones, implying female authors' greater pessimism in private texts. However, in public texts, female authors demonstrated no significant difference in sentiment scores compared with their male counterparts, suggesting a similar level of optimism between genders in these texts.

In order to explore the possible reason for this inconsistency, I went back to the public texts, namely, WeChat articles. Upon reviewing the texts, most female authors wrote on neutral daily life topics such as reading, learning skills, fashion, and health. Conversely, male-authored texts tended to focus on hotly debated topics like COVID-19 restrictions, the Ukraine war, and social injustice. Compared with male-authored topics, female-authored topics present fewer opportunities to elicit intense negative emotions. Whether this preference for different types of topics is conscious or unconscious remains unknown.

Furthermore, interestingly and unexpectedly, the results showed that the male authors, especially younger male authors, displayed the significantly highest sentiment scores in Online Chat texts, which suggests that they are more positive in the interactive communication than monologue or soliloquy. This finding aligns with previous studies suggesting men are more dependent on social interaction and its support (Caetano et al., 2013). Specifically, Caetano et al. (2013) found that low social network involvement is closely associated with poor self-rated health in older men and older men's mental health is associated with emotional support from close relations. They spend less time alone and have more people to count on to get social support (Caetano et al., 2013, p. 12). This may suggest that men are more likely to be dependent on social interaction and the support from which it arises. Therefore, it is much more likely that they are supposed to be more supportive and thus more positive towards others in the social interaction in order to get the same support from others. In addition, societal expectations might encourage men to disguise unpleasant emotions and appear more optimistic to garner more support from others (Fiorentini, 2013). Specifically, he believed that males learn to disguise and cover their emotions more than women because they are socialised differently. This suggests that in interactive social communications, they tend to disguise their true selves and mask their unpleasant emotions and try to be more optimistic towards others in order to get more likes and support.

Regarding age, it is worth mentioning that even though statistical results did not indicate a significant difference in sentiment scores between the younger and older authors, there is a clear trend in both private and public writings: the younger authors tend to have higher standard deviations (SD = 90.51 in private texts and SD = 63.76 in public texts) in their sentiment scores than the older authors (SD = 69.90 in private texts and SD = 50.20 in public texts). This suggests greater variation or diversity within the sentiment scores of younger authors, a trend that aligns with the notion that people become more emotionally stable as they age (Pennebaker, 2011a). This is mainly because older people have had more time to develop and refine their emotional regulation skills (Pennebaker, 2011a). Over time, they might have learned to better understand and manage their emotions, allowing them to cope more effectively with stressful or challenging situations.

There are also other factors that might contribute to increased emotional stability in older age, such as a greater sense of perspective, a more positive outlook on life (Pennebaker, 2011a), and increased social support from family and friends (Pennebaker, 2011a). A more positive outlook in older people could be supported by the results in the context of private texts only. The possible reason is that people tend to disguise less, be more authentic and show their true selves in private context, which is similar to the above-mentioned situation of gender. Additionally, changes in brain chemistry and structure that occur as we age might also play a role in promoting emotional stability.

Notably, the same tendency was observed between the female and male authors. In other words, in both private and public writings, female authors tend to have higher standard deviations (SD = 73.53 in private texts and SD = 60.71 in public texts) in their sentiment scores than male authors (SD = 54.03 in private texts and SD = 52.50 in public texts). This parallel between female and young authors will be further discussed in Section 3.3, in which possible style matching between younger and female authors will be elaborated upon in light of a similar tendency in the use of personal pronouns and graduations.

3.1.3 Experiment 3: Distinctiveness of Keywords

The literature review suggests that keywords could be the indicators of 'about-ness' (Bondi & Scott, 2010) and style (Bondi & Scott, 2010; Scott & Tribble, 2006; Taylor & Marchi, 2018). In particular, 'aboutness' generally involves content words closely associated with the topics of texts. Given that text topics can significantly vary, comparing aboutness-related keywords between texts proves challenging. Consequently, only function keywords indicative of style, such as personal pronouns (Scott & Tribble, 2006; Zhou, 2007), exclamations, and adverbial graduations (Martin & White, 2005) which include intensifiers (Zhou, 2007), were analysed. In Chinese, it is generally accepted that personal pronouns, exclamations, and adverbs are all classified as function words (Zhang, 2022). This differs from English, where adverbs are categorised as content words.

In addition, as noted in Section 2.1, only the top 10 keywords (selected based on the four-term Log-Likelihood keyness measure and $p < 0.05$ with Bonferroni correction) from each author's texts were included in the analysis. This ensures that all analysed keywords are significantly prominent words, which means that their presence or absence carries more weight than their frequency of use. A binary logistic regression analysis was then conducted to explore the relationship between these keywords (specifically, personal pronouns, exclamations, and graduations) and the gender and age of the text authors.

I investigated the predictive power of these keyword features (as predictor variables) in determining the gender and age of the authors (the outcome variable). Conversely, I also examined the predictive power of gender and age (as predictor variables) using these keywords (the outcome variable). The results established a reverse bidirectional causality between the keywords and the demographic background information, specifically age and gender, indicating a strong correlation between these variables.

1) Distinctiveness of keywords in predicting gender

The results demonstrate that the logistic regression model for predicting gender proved significant, $\chi^2(3, N = 114) = 27.87, p < .001$ for Omnibus tests, and $p = .510$ for the Hosmer–Lemeshow test. This result indicates that the predictor variables (i.e., personal pronouns, exclamations, and graduations) collectively explained a significant amount of variance in the outcome variable (i.e., gender of text authors). More precisely, the model explains 29.3% (Nagelkerke R Square) of the variance in gender and correctly classified 70.2% of the cases.

In more detail, the results in Figure 21 reveal that firstly, male authors (target) were ten times more likely to avoid using personal pronouns than to use them [$OR = 9.828$, 95%CI (2.719, 35.522)]. In other words, for male authors, the ratio of not using to using personal pronouns was 9.828. Secondly, male authors were nearly three times more likely to avoid using exclamations than to use them [$OR = 2.837$, 95%CI (1.065, 7.560)]. In other words, for the male authors, the ratio of not using exclamations to using them was 2.837. Thirdly, male authors were five times more likely to avoid using graduations than to use them [$OR = 5.09$, 95%CI (1.856, 13.959)]. In other words, for male authors, the ratio of not using graduations to using them was 5.09.

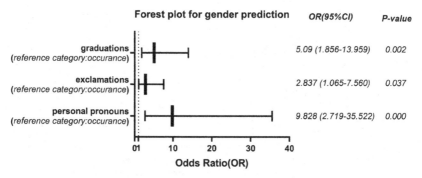

Figure 21 Distinctiveness of keywords in gender

2) Distinctiveness of keywords in predicting age

The logistic regression model for predicting age was also significant, $\chi^2(3, N = 114) = 15.68$, $p = .001$ for Omnibus tests, and $p = .533$ for the Hosmer–Lemeshow test, indicating that the predictor variables (i.e., personal pronouns, exclamations, and graduations) collectively explained a significant amount of variance in the outcome variable (i.e., the age of text authors). Precisely, the model explained 17.2% (Nagelkerke R Square) of the variance in gender and correctly predicted 64.0% of the cases.

A detailed analysis of Figure 22 reveals, firstly, that older authors (target) were nearly five times more likely to avoid using personal pronouns than to use them [$OR = 4.673$, 95%CI (1.484, 14.715)]. In other words, for older authors, the ratio of not using personal pronouns to using them was 4.673. Secondly, older authors were three times more likely to avoid using graduations than to use them [$OR = 3.142$, 95%CI (1.297, 7.609)]. In other words, for older authors, the ratio of not using graduations to using them was 3.142. However, there was no significant association between the use of exclamations and the author's gender ($p = .681$).

From these results, it can be inferred that personal pronouns, exclamations, and graduations are all distinctive in predicting an author's gender, but only personal pronouns and graduations were distinctive in predicting the author's age.

However, the identified targets in the two regression tests were only the male authors and the older authors (the larger coded group is identified as the 'target'). Thus, the specific gender differences between females and males, and age differences between younger and older authors in terms of the distinctive keyword features remain unclear. To address these detailed gender and age differences, two more logistic regression analyses were conducted with the outcome variables and predictor variables interchanged, as the

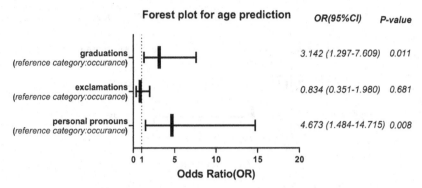

Figure 22 Distinctiveness of keywords in age

original predictor variables are also binary. This approach facilitated a more thorough investigation of the correlations.

3) The detailed correlation between gender, age, and personal pronoun

The logistic regression model demonstrating the gender and age differences in terms of predicting the use of personal pronouns proved significant, with $\chi^2(2, N = 114) = 18.616$, $p < .001$ for Omnibus tests, and $p = .816$ for the Hosmer–Lemeshow test. The results indicate that the predictor variables (i.e., gender and age) collectively explained a significant amount of variance in the outcome variable (i.e., the use of personal pronouns). The model accounted for 25.4% (Nagelkerke R Square) of the variance in personal pronoun usage and accurately classified 83.3% of the cases.

Figure 23 reveals that firstly, personal pronouns were six times more likely to be used by the female authors than the male authors [$OR = 6.387$, 95%CI (1.909, 21.372)]. In other words, the female authors were six times more likely to use personal pronouns than the male authors. Secondly, personal pronouns were three times more likely to be used by the younger authors than the older authors [$OR = 3.288$, 95%CI (1.035, 10.452)]. In other words, younger authors were three times more likely to use personal pronouns than older ones.

4) The detailed correlation between gender, age, and graduation

The results from the logistic regression model highlighted significant gender and age differences in predicting the use of graduations, with $\chi^2(2, N = 114) = 13.439$, $p = .001$ for Omnibus tests, and $p = .081$ for the Hosmer–Lemeshow test. This suggests that the predictor variables (i.e., gender and age) collectively explained a significant portion of the variance in the outcome variable (i.e., the use of

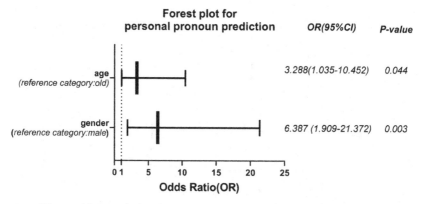

Figure 23 Correlation between gender, age, and personal pronoun

graduations). Specifically, the model explained 15.3% (Nagelkerke R Square) of the variance in personal pronoun usage and correctly classified 71.9% of the cases.

As shown in Figure 24, firstly, graduations were nearly three times as likely to be used by the female authors compared with the male authors [$OR = 2.907$, 95%CI (1.188, 7.115)], suggesting that female authors were three times more likely to use graduations than their male counterparts. Secondly, graduations were almost three times as likely to be used by the younger authors compared with the older authors [$OR = 2.59$, 95%CI (1.098, 6.111)], indicating that younger authors were three times more likely to use graduations than the older authors. However, there was no significant association between the author's gender ($p = .122$) and age ($p = .195$) differences in relation to the use of exclamations alone.

5) Discussion for gender difference

Overall, personal pronouns, exclamations, and graduations, either individually or collectively, effectively predict an author's gender. More specifically, it is projected that female authors tend to use more personal pronouns, exclamations, and graduations than female authors.

The findings align with previous studies on gender differences in the use of pronouns (Pennebaker, 2011a; Säily et al., 2011; Tannen,1991; Tausczik & Pennebaker, 2010; Zhou, 2007), showing that females are more likely to use more intensifiers (one type of graduations) and personal pronouns than males. They also support the notion that men's communication style tends to be more informational, while women's is more interactive and involved, which inevitably leads to more frequent use of personal pronouns (Biber et al., 1998; Pennebaker, 2011a; Rayson et al., 1997; Säily et al., 2011).

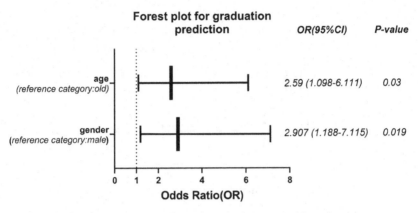

Figure 24 Correlation between gender, age, and graduation

More specifically, females tend to use more social words and pronouns (Pennebaker, 2011a; Tausczik & Pennebaker, 2010), and view matters from the perspective of human relationships, demonstrating understanding and empathy by sharing personal experiences (Zhou, 2007). Personal pronouns, such as '我(I)', '我们(we)', and '你(you)', are frequently used when sharing personal experiences and emotions (Pennebaker, 2011a; Tausczik & Pennebaker, 2010) because they refer to the speakers or writers themselves and the listeners or readers. Indeed, the use of personal pronouns is often essential for conveying the personal nature of shared experiences, distinguishing them from hypothetical or generalised situations.

In the context of human relationships, personal pronouns enable us to establish connections, express empathy, and build trust with others. This explains why they are frequently used in discussions related to human relationships. Especially the first-person pronoun, such as 'we', is frequently used for rapport building (Tannen, 1991) in relationships.

Furthermore, showing understanding and sympathy may involve not only personal pronouns, but also exclamations and graduations as they're closely related to expressing emotions and feelings (Zhou, 2007). Exclamations are words or phrases that express strong emotions or feelings, and are typically punctuated with an exclamation mark (!) to highlight the intensity of the conveyed emotion. Examples of exclamations include '哦(o)', '呀(ya)', '啊(a)', and '哈(ha)'. Consistent with the more emotional tendency of females (Pennebaker, 2011a; Pennebaker et al., 2003; Latu et al., 2013; Ruberg & Steenbergh, 2011), it is natural for female authors to use more exclamations in their writing and communication.

As for graduation, it is an important aspect of appraisal because it allows speakers to convey subtle differences in their social attitudes and beliefs, and to convey their stance towards the subject matter in a more nuanced and sophisticated way (Martin & White, 2005). It is a key element in creating evaluative meanings that are contextually appropriate and reflect the speaker's individual viewpoint (Martin & White, 2005). Graduations are closely associated with women's social interests (Pennebaker, 2011a; Tausczik & Pennebaker, 2010) and their more involved and interactive tendencies (Biber et al., 1998; Rayson et al., 1997; Säily et al., 2011; Zhou, 2007). Specifically, a greater use of graduations might suggest the use of intensive adverbs to indicate the degree or intensity of a particular evaluative category (Newman et al., 2008).

Notably, force, one of the two types of graduation (which includes both intensification and quantification), can increase or decrease the 'volume' of the involved attitude. Thus, force has an impact on social alignment and solidarity. When the attitude is upscaled (made more forceful), it tends to portray the speakers or writers as strongly involved themselves in the expressed value position. This, in turn, may align the reader or audience more closely with that value position.

In summary, graduations can shape the reader's perception of the speaker or writer's attitude and alignment with a particular value position. The more forceful the language, the more strongly the speaker or writer is seen as committed to that position, and the more likely the audience or reader is to align with it. Consistent with the greater social interests (Pennebaker, 2011a; Tausczik & Pennebaker, 2010) and more involved or interactive tendency (Biber et al., 1998; Rayson et al., 1997; Säily et al., 2011) of women, it is not surprising that they are more likely to use graduations than men.

6) Discussion for age difference

Compared to the predictive power for gender, personal pronouns, exclamations, and graduations are less strongly associated with an author's age. Age is a more complex and intriguing social factor than gender because gender is usually stable, while age changes throughout our lives (Pennebaker, 2011a). In spite of this, based on the results, the age of text authors could still be correctly predicted by some keyword features, especially personal pronouns and graduations.

The results indicate that younger authors (born around and after the year 2000) are more likely to use personal pronouns and graduations than older authors (born around and before the year 1980). The results are consistent with prior findings that younger individuals, such as teenagers, tend to use personal pronouns, such as 'I' and 'you', more frequently (Pennebaker, 2011a). Conversely, the older the people become, the more likely they are to use bigger words, prepositions, and articles (Pennebaker, 2011a). Similarly, the results also support the findings that people use fewer self-references as they age (Pennebaker & Stone, 2003), and thus their use of 'first-personal singular decreased with time' (Tausczik & Pennebaker, 2010, p. 36) as people become less self-focused with increasing age (Pennebaker & Stone, 2003).

As for graduations or intensifiers, as mentioned previously, in most cases, they are used to convey strong and intensified emotions and feelings. The findings are consistent with the concept that 'intensifying words are generally used and created by young people' (Bordet, 2015, p. 6), and that younger people tend to use more intensifiers than their older counterparts.

There are a few possible explanations for this age-related disparity. One possibility is that younger people, akin to females, may use language in a more emotional or expressive manner (Pennebaker, 2011a), and intensifiers serve to articulate these emotions effectively. Additionally, and similar to females, younger people may be more inclined to use intensifiers as a marker of their affiliation with a specific social group or subculture (Bordet, 2015). In my analysis, typical observed examples of such intensifier usage include '超(extremely)' and '狠(very)'. Notably, the use of '狠(very)' is actually a creative misuse and reinterpretation of '很 (very)', a linguistic style often adopted by young people as a fashionable use of intensifiers.

However, it is essential to acknowledge that individual differences and contextual factors can also play a role in the use of graduations or intensifiers. For instance, some older people may use intensifiers frequently, while some younger people may use them sparingly. Overall, the relationship between the use of graduations and age is complex and multifaceted, and more research is needed to fully understand it.

3.1.4 Summary for Authorship Profiling

Based on the findings, several key insights into authorship profiling have emerged. Firstly, an author's gender can be inferred from the sentiment scores of their texts. More specifically, sentiment scores can effectively predict the gender within a given genre or predict the genre within a given gender, highlighting the interactive effect of gender and genre on the sentiment scores of the texts.

On the one hand, in most instances, particularly in private writings, the results indicate that the lower the sentiment scores (roughly ranging from +59 to –70 or lower) are, the more likely the authors are females. On the other hand, the higher the sentiment scores (roughly ranging from +70 to +307 or higher) are, the more likely the authors are males. However, these tendencies can vary in public writings depending on the topics discussed.

Secondly, in interactive peer communications, higher sentiment scores (roughly ranging from 122 to 370 or higher) are generally indicative of male authors.

Thirdly, the use of keywords, which include personal pronouns, exclamations, and graduations, has proven to be effective predictors of both an author's gender and age. While these elements are more potent indicators of gender, they also bear relevance to the age of authors. In the context of gender, it is evident that female authors typically use more personal pronouns, exclamations, and graduations than male authors do. Regarding age, it is more closely associated with personal pronouns and graduations. In particular, personal pronouns and graduations are associated with younger authors (born around and after 2000), who tend to use them more frequently than older authors (born around and before 1980).

In summary, the preceding results affirm that features such as sentiment expression and the use of keywords like personal pronouns, exclamations, and graduations are indicative of an author's unique writing style and habits. This is in line with research that combines sentiment features as part of an author's writing style (Martins et al., 2021), and the corpus linguistic studies that categorise personal pronouns, exclamations, and graduations as the style indicators among keywords (Bondi & Scott, 2010; Scott & Tribble, 2006; Taylor & Marchi, 2018; Zhou, 2007).

All the tested distinctive profiling features (sentiment scores, personal pronouns, exclamations, and graduations) were subsequently evaluated as a collective feature set to test their potential attribution power in the authorship attribution experiment discussed in the next section.

3.2 Research Question 2: Authorship Attribution

3.2.1 Experiment 4: Attribution Strength of Sentiment Scores and Keywords

The main purpose of this section is to test the potential attribution power of the aforementioned profiling features. More specifically, the design of this section seeks to answer two main questions. Firstly, are the sentiment and keyword features distinctive enough to attribute authors compared to other well-established features? Secondly, are there situations in which these sentiment and keyword features might outperform the well-established features?

In order to explore the two questions, a reference feature set composed of well-established and frequently used lexico-syntactic features was constructed. These features include word length, type token ratio, sentence length (in terms of the Chinese characters), and Chinese character n-gram (n = 1–4).

The choice of a one- to four-character n-gram range is twofold. Firstly, it is a generally accepted fact that the majority of Chinese words are composed of one to four Chinese characters, despite there being exceptions. Roughly 85% of Chinese words are composed of one to three characters (Zang et al., 2018), and most commonly used Chinese words typically fall within the range of one to four characters range. Secondly, even though the exceptions with longer words could be crucial for distinguishing different authors and may excel in attribution, this section aims to treat the lexico-syntactic feature set as a reference feature set for comparison with the sentiment scores and keyword features. Therefore, the reference feature set should encompass an equivalent number of features, namely, seven. As a result, only the most established and frequently used features, such as the Chinese character n-gram (n = 1–4) were selected for the reference lexico-syntactic feature set.

The target feature set comprises sentiment scores and keyword features. More accurately, the keyword features include personal pronouns, exclamations, and graduations. Given the limited number of personal pronouns, these features were generated separately, which include '我 (I/me)', '你 (you)', '他 (he/him)', and '她 (she/her)'. In Chinese, personal pronouns do not vary based on their role in a sentence. Consequently, there is no distinction between nominative and accusative pronouns, unlike in certain other languages. The same pronoun is utilised regardless of whether it serves as the subject or the object in a sentence.

The lexico-syntactic feature set includes word length, type token ratio, sentence length (in terms of the Chinese characters), and Chinese character n-gram (n = 1–4). Both feature sets are listed in Table 2.

Therefore, with an equal number of features, these two feature sets are approximately comparable.

Check for Basic Assumptions of Discriminant Analysis

Discriminant analysis is a statistical method employed to classify cases or texts into groups guided by a set of predictor variables. The assumptions for discriminant analysis encompass feature reliability, outliers, the number of predictor variables in each attribution model, multivariate normality within groups, and homogeneity of variance-covariance matrices (Tabachnick and Fidell, 2007). However, it is important to note that violating certain assumptions does not necessarily invalidate the discriminant analysis results. On the one hand, discriminant analysis tends to be robust against violations of the normality and the homogeneity of variance-covariance matrices when sample sizes are equal (Tabachnick & Fidell, 2007). In this authorship attribution experiment, each

Table 2 Two feature sets for authorship attribution tests

Target feature set Sentiment and keyword features (7)	Reference feature set Lexico-syntactic features (7)
Sentiment scores	Word length
exclamations	Type token ratio
graduation	Sentence length
Personal pronouns:	n-gram:
我 (I/me)	One-character/letter words
你 (you)	Two-character/letter words
他 (he/him)	Three-character/letter words
她 (she/her)	Four-character/letter words

Note: All the listed features are normalised per 1,000 characters.

author's texts were segmented into 15 smaller texts, ensuring an equal sample size for each author.

On the other hand, discriminant analysis is highly sensitive to outliers, and the size of the smallest group must exceed the number of predictor variables. Therefore, basic assumptions, which include feature reliability, outlier, and number of predictor variables were checked and reported. This aligns with the experiment's primary objective of testing the feasibility of using the distinctive profiling features in attribution tasks through comparison with well-established features.

1) Feature reliability
All the lexico-syntactic features were generated using WordSmith Tools 8.0.

The sentiment scores and keyword features were generated using Python, specifically through pysenti 0.1.7, which was introduced earlier. Exclamations, graduations, and personal pronouns were identified and calculated. Exclamation words (including exclamation marks) were derived from a detailed examination of the texts, keyword lists, and the most frequently used Chinese exclamation words (Zhang, 2022). In total, 11 exclamation words were analysed, which include '哦(o)', '噢(ao)', '呀(ya)', '啊(a)', '哈(ha)', '哇(wa)','吖(ya)', '唉 (ai)', '哼(heng)', '啊喂(awe)', and '呵呵(hehe)'. Graduations were derived from an intricate analysis of the texts, keywords list, and English appraisal system (Martin & White, 2005). In total, 11 graduations were analysed, which include '很(very)', '非常(very)', '还(still)', '有点(a little)', '真(really)', '完全 (totally)', '贼(extremely)', '正(exactly)', '超(extremely)', '的确(indeed)', and '狠(very)'. Personal pronouns were derived from the keyword lists. In total, four personal pronouns were analysed, which include '我(I/me)', '你(you)', '他 (he/him)', and '她(she/her)'.

2) Outlier
Each group was subjected to data screening to ensure the absence of extreme outliers.

3) Number of predictor variables
In the attribution tests, each author's texts were segmented into 15 smaller pieces for discriminant analysis. Depending on the two mentioned feature sets, among all the following attribution tests, the maximum feature set included 14 predictor variables/features (when both feature sets were used simultaneously for attribution) and the minimum feature set contained seven predictor variables/features (when each feature set was used separately and independently). Thus, the number of features utilised in each test was less than the sample size of each author texts group (15 texts for each author), which means that the assumption regarding the number of predictor variables is met.

Indicators of the Discriminant Effect of Feature Set

The discriminant effect of a feature set signifies the extent to which the features in the set are able to distinguish between different groups in a classification task. The following are several indicators gauging the discriminant effect of a feature set:

1) Wilks's lambda and eigenvalue
Both Wilks's lambda and eigenvalue serve as indicators of the significance of the discriminant function of a feature set (Cigic & Bugarski, 2010; Zhang, 2016). Wilks's lambda, specifically, represents the proportion of the total variance in the discriminant scores that is not accounted for by differences among groups. Therefore, the value of Wilks' lambda, ranging from 0 to 1, should ideally be as small as possible; smaller values suggest a stronger discriminatory power of the independent or predictor variables. In other words, a lower Wilks' lambda value indicates that the groups are more distinct and are better separated by the predictor variables or features.

Moreover, to evaluate the significance of the differences between groups in discriminant analysis, the observed value of Wilks' lambda is expected to be smaller than the critical value, namely 0.05.

Conversely, the eigenvalue indicates the discriminant function's effectiveness in differentiating groups. Larger eigenvalues denote superior discriminant function. The 'Kaiser criterion' is a common method to evaluate eigenvalues, suggesting retention of eigenvalues greater than 1 (Michalos, 2014).

2) Original accuracy rate and cross-validated accuracy rate

Original accuracy refers to the performance of a model on the same dataset it was trained on, while cross-validated accuracy refers to the performance of a model on unseen or new data. Specifically, in the authorship attribution, both types of accuracy rates assess the effectiveness of the feature sets in distinguishing between groups of author texts. Particularly, the cross-validated accuracy rate provides a more truthful reflection of the discriminant function's power than the original rate (Burns & Burns, 2008).

3) Significance evaluation of the accuracy rate

The accuracy rate is statistically significant if it surpasses the proportion achieved by chance (Zhang, 2004). The expected criterion is $(100\%/G)*1.2$ or 1.25, with G representing the number of authors (Zhang, 2004, p. 264). For instance, in an 18-author discriminant analysis, if both the original and cross-validated accuracy rate exceed the expected criteria of 41.7% $(100\%/18*1.25)$, it would be reasonable to state that the observed accuracy rate is significantly higher than what would be expected by chance.

Data

The authorship attribution tests were conducted on the Diaries, Blogs, and Moments, namely type I texts. These data were selected for two reasons. Firstly, it represents one of the most populous groups in terms of author diversity, thereby increasing the complexity and challenge of the authorship attribution task and enhancing the reliability of the test results. Secondly, this type of data comprises several sub-genres of texts, making the attribution task more complicated and challenging, thereby potentially boosting the reliability and validity of the results. Thirdly, the punctuations in this data type are used normally and conventionally, enabling the calculation of the 'sentence length' feature. By contrast, the punctuations in Online Chats (type II texts) are often omitted, especially periods, which makes the calculation of 'sentence length' extremely difficult, if not impossible. Therefore, the authorship attribution tests were only conducted on the private type I texts which include Diaries, Blogs, and Moments.

Based on the data and the two feature sets, the authorship attribution tests were carried out from within-group tests to between-group tests based on different gender groups, age groups, and their combined groups. More specifically, nine tests were conducted: younger females group (18 authors), older females group (5 authors), younger males group (6 authors), older males group (6 authors), all females group (23 authors), all males group (12 authors), all younger authors group (24 authors), all older authors group (11 authors), and all author combined group which includes all 35 authors.

Each subsequent attribution test comprises three tables, demonstrating the results of the lexico-syntactic feature set, the sentiment and keyword feature set, and their combined feature set, respectively. More specifically, the results of each feature set include the number of authors, number of predictors, discriminant functions, eigenvalue, Wilks' lambda, significance of the functions, original accuracy rate, and cross-validated accuracy rate.

Sentiment Scores and Keywords in the Authorship Attribution of Younger Females

In the attribution of the 18 younger females, the sentiment scores and keyword feature set surpassed the performance of the lexico-syntactic feature set. Furthermore, their combined effectiveness also exceeded their separate capabilities.

According to the attribution results of the lexico-syntactic feature set for the younger females (see Table 3), all of the seven eigenvalues indicate weak discriminant functions (eigenvalue < 1). The results of Wilks's lambda show that five of the seven functions are significant ($p < .05$). Overall, both the original and cross-validated accuracy rates provided statistically significant evidence of the model's ability to predict outcomes. These rates were markedly higher than the proportional by-chance accuracy rate of 6.9% (100%/18*1.25).

In the attribution results of the sentiment scores and keyword feature set for the younger females (see Table 4), one of the seven eigenvalues indicates a strong discriminant function (eigenvalue > 1). The results of Wilks's lambda show that five of the seven functions were significant ($p < .05$). Consequently, both the original and cross-validated accuracy rates provided statistically significant evidence of the model's ability to predict outcomes. These rates were considerably larger than the proportional by-chance accuracy rate, which stands at 6.9% (100%/18*1.25).

The results from the combined feature set (see Table 5) indicate that 2 out of the 14 eigenvalues showed strong discriminant functions (eigenvalue > 1). Wilks's lambda reveals that 7 out of the 14 functions were significant ($p < .05$). Accordingly, both the original and cross-validated accuracy rates provided statistically significant evidence of the model's ability to predict outcomes. These rates were much larger than the proportional by-chance accuracy rate, which is 6.9% (100%/18*1.25).

Based on these results, it is clear that in the attribution of the 18 younger female authors, the sentiment and keyword feature set outperformed the lexico-syntactic

Table 3 Attribution results of lexico-syntactic feature set for younger females

Number of authors	Number of predictors	Functions	Eigenvalue	Wilks' lambda	Sig. of function	OAR (%)	CVAR (%)
18	7	Function 1	.888	.147	.000	28.5	22.6
		Function 2	.771	.277	.000		
		Function 3	.357	.490	.000		
		Function 4	.200	.665	.000		
		Function 5	.141	.798	.026		
		Function 6	.062	.910	.452		
		Function 7	.035	.967	.646		

Note: Sig. = significance; OAR = original accuracy rate; CVAR = cross-validated accuracy rate.

Table 4 Attribution results of sentiment and keyword feature set for younger females

Number of authors	Number of predictors	Functions	Eigenvalue	Wilks' lambda	Sig. of function	OAR (%)	CVAR (%)
18	7	Function 1	1.005	.151	.000	38.9	28.5
		Function 2	.525	.302	.000		
		Function 3	.407	.461	.000		
		Function 4	.213	.648	.000		
		Function 5	.165	.787	.001		
		Function 6	.073	.917	.071		
		Function 7	.017	.984	.300		

Note: Sig. = significance; OAR = original accuracy rate; CVAR = cross-validated accuracy rate.

Table 5 Attribution results of combined feature set for younger females

Number of authors	Number of predictors	Functions	Eigenvalue	Wilks' lambda	Sig. of function	OAR (%)	CVAR (%)
18	14	Function 1	1.467	.029	.000	46.7	31.9
		Function 2	1.143	.072	.000		
		Function 3	.803	.155	.000		
		Function 4	.459	.280	.000		
		Function 5	.287	.408	.000		
		Function 6	.224	.526	.001		
		Function 7	.145	.643	.046		
		Function 8	.119	.737	.256		
		Function 9	.104	.825	.675		
		Function 10	.039	.910	.980		
		Function 11	.032	.945	.986		
		Function 12	.016	.976	.995		
		Function 13	.007	.991	.994		
		Function 14	.002	.998	.975		

Note: Sig. = significance; OAR = original accuracy rate; CVAR = cross-validated accuracy rate.

feature set. In addition, the combined feature set surpassed the performance of the individual feature set, which implied that both feature sets contributed positively to the authorship attribution of the 18 younger female authors. Interestingly, the combined strength of the two feature sets seemed to exceed the sum of the strengths of each individual group in terms of the number of larger eigenvalues.

Sentiment Scores and Keywords in the Authorship Attribution of Older Females

In the case of attributing the five older females, the lexico-syntactic feature set outperformed the sentiment and keyword feature set. The combined strength of these two feature sets also surpassed their individual performances.

According to the attribution results of the lexico-syntactic feature set for the older females (Table 6), one of the four eigenvalues suggested a strong discriminant function (eigenvalue > 1). Wilks's lambda results revealed that three out of the four functions were significant ($p < .05$). Subsequently, both the original and cross-validated accuracy rates provided statistically significant evidence of the model's ability to predict outcomes. These rates were much larger than the proportional by-chance accuracy rate of 25% (100%/5*1.25).

According to the attribution results of the sentiment and keyword feature set for the older females (Table 7), all of the four eigenvalues suggested weak discriminant functions (eigenvalue < 1). The results of Wilks's lambda showed that two of the four functions were significant ($p < .05$). Both the original and cross-validated accuracy rates provided statistically significant evidence of the model's ability to predict outcomes. These rates were considerably larger than the proportional by-chance accuracy rate, which is 25% (100%/5*1.25).

The results from the combined feature set (see Table 8) showed that two of the four eigenvalues suggested strong discriminant functions (eigenvalue > 1). Wilks's lambda results indicated that three of the four functions were significant ($p < .05$). Accordingly, both the original and cross-validated accuracy rates provided statistically significant evidence of the model's ability to predict outcomes, exceeding the proportional by-chance accuracy rate of 25% (100%/5*1.25) by a substantial margin.

Based on these results, it is clear that in attributing the five older female authors, the lexico-syntactic feature set outperformed the sentiment and keyword feature set. In addition, the combined feature set outperformed the individual feature sets, which suggested that both feature sets positively contributed to the attribution of the five older female authors. Furthermore, the combined strength of the two feature sets seemed to surpass the sum of the strengths of each individual group in terms of the number of larger eigenvalues.

Table 6 Attribution results of lexico-syntactic feature set for older females

Number of authors	Number of predictors	Functions	Eigenvalue	Wilks' lambda	Sig. of function	OAR (%)	CVAR (%)
5	7	Function 1	1.697	.139	.000	72.2	63.9
		Function 2	.765	.375	.000		
		Function 3	.350	.663	.003		
		Function 4	.118	.895	.124		

Note: Sig. = significance; OAR = original accuracy rate; CVAR = cross-validated accuracy rate.

Table 7 Attribution results of sentiment and keyword feature set for older females

Number of authors	Number of predictors	Functions	Eigenvalue	Wilks' lambda	Sig. of function	OAR (%)	CVAR (%)
5	7	Function 1	.396	.423	.001	51.4	36.1
		Function 2	.380	.591	.012		
		Function 3	.147	.816	.210		
		Function 4	.069	.936	.366		

Note: Sig. = significance; OAR = original accuracy rate; CVAR = cross-validated accuracy rate.

Table 8 Attribution results of combined feature set for older females

Number of authors	Number of predictors	Functions	Eigenvalue	Wilks' lambda	Sig. of function	OAR (%)	CVAR (%)
5	14	Function 1	2.304	.063	.000	77.8	61.1
		Function 2	1.190	.209	.000		
		Function 3	.629	.457	.002		
		Function 4	.343	.744	.078		

Note: Sig. = significance; OAR = original accuracy rate; CVAR = cross-validated accuracy rate.

Sentiment Scores and Keywords in the Authorship Attribution of Younger Males

In attributing the authorship of the six younger males, the lexico-syntactic feature set outperformed the sentiment and keyword feature set. Furthermore, the combined strength of these two feature sets surpassed their individual performances.

According to the attribution results of the lexico-syntactic feature set for the younger males (see Table 9), two of the five eigenvalues indicated very strong discriminant functions (eigenvalue > 1). The results of Wilks's lambda revealed that three of the five functions were significant ($p < .05$). Accordingly, both the original and cross-validated accuracy rates provided statistically significant evidence of the model's ability to predict outcomes, far surpassing the proportional by-chance accuracy rate of 20.8% (100%/6*1.25).

According to the attribution results of the sentiment and keyword feature set for the younger males (see Table 10), one of the five eigenvalues indicated a strong discriminant function (eigenvalue > 1). The results of Wilks's lambda showed that four of the five functions were significant ($p < .05$). Accordingly, both the original and the cross-validated accuracy rates provided statistically significant evidence of the model's ability to predict outcomes, significantly exceeding the proportional by-chance accuracy rate, which is 20.8% (100%/6*1.25).

The results of the combined feature set (Table 11) show that three of the five eigenvalues indicated very strong discriminant functions (eigenvalue > 1). Wilks's lambda results showed that all of the five functions were significant ($p < .05$). Accordingly, both the original and cross-validated accuracy rates provided statistically significant evidence of the model's ability to predict outcomes, greatly exceeding the proportional by-chance accuracy rate of 20.8% (100%/6*1.25).

Based on these results, it is clear that in the attribution of the six younger male authors, the lexico-syntactic feature set outperformed the sentiment and keyword feature set. In addition, the combined feature set outperformed the individual feature sets, which suggested that both feature sets positively contributed to the attribution of the six younger male authors.

Sentiment Scores and Keywords in the Authorship Attribution of Older Males

For the attribution of the six older males, the lexico-syntactic feature set outperformed the sentiment and keyword feature set. Furthermore, the combined strength of these features also outshone their individual performances.

Table 9 Attribution results of lexico-syntactic feature set for younger males

Number of authors	Number of predictors	Functions	Eigenvalue	Wilks' lambda	Sig. of function	OAR (%)	CVAR (%)
6	7	Function 1	7.284	.019	.000	84.4	74.4
		Function 2	2.656	.157	.000		
		Function 3	.486	.575	.000		
		Function 4	.118	.854	.113		
		Function 5	.046	.956	.290		

Note: Sig. = significance; OAR = original accuracy rate; CVAR = cross-validated accuracy rate.

Table 10 Attribution results of sentiment and keyword feature set for younger males

Number of authors	Number of predictors	Functions	Eigenvalue	Wilks' lambda	Sig. of function	OAR (%)	CVAR (%)
6	7	Function 1	3.499	.076	.000	68.9	61.1
		Function 2	.557	.340	.000		
		Function 3	.382	.529	.000		
		Function 4	.307	.731	.001		
		Function 5	.046	.956	.292		

Note: Sig. = significance; OAR = original accuracy rate; CVAR = cross-validated accuracy rate.

Table 11 Attribution results of combined feature set for younger males

Number of authors	Number of predictors	Functions	Eigenvalue	Wilks' lambda	Sig. of function	OAR (%)	CVAR (%)
6	14	Function 1	7.588	.003	.000	93.3	80.0
		Function 2	3.495	.026	.000		
		Function 3	2.826	.118	.000		
		Function 4	.565	.450	.000		
		Function 5	.420	.704	.002		

Note: Sig. = significance; OAR = original accuracy rate; CVAR = cross-validated accuracy rate.

According to the attribution results of the lexico-syntactic feature set for the older males (see Table 12), two of the five eigenvalues indicated strong discriminant functions (eigenvalue > 1). Additionally, the results of Wilks's lambda indicated that four of the five functions were significant (p < .05). Accordingly, both the original and cross-validated accuracy rates provided statistically significant evidence of the model's ability to predict outcomes, exceeding the proportional by-chance accuracy rate of 20.8% (100%/6*1.25).

According to the attribution results of sentiment and keyword feature set for the older males (see Table 13), one of the five eigenvalues suggested a strong discriminant function (eigenvalue > 1). The results of Wilks's lambda indicated that three of the five functions were significant (p < .05). Accordingly, both the original and the cross-validated accuracy rates provided statistically significant evidence of the model's ability to predict outcomes, exceeding markedly the proportional by-chance accuracy rate of 20.8% (100%/6*1.25).

The results of the combined feature set (see Table 14) show that three of the five eigenvalues indicated very strong discriminant functions (eigenvalue > 1). Wilks's lambda results indicated that all of the five functions were significant (p < .05). Accordingly, both the original and cross-validated accuracy rates provided statistically significant evidence of the model's ability to predict outcomes, considerably exceeding the proportional by-chance accuracy rate, which is 20.8% (100%/6*1.25).

Based on the preceding results, it is obvious that in the attribution of the six older male authors, the lexico-syntactic feature set outperformed the sentiment and keyword feature set. In addition, the combined feature set outperformed the individual feature sets, which suggested that both feature sets were making their positive contributions to the attribution of the six older male authors.

Sentiment Scores and Keywords in the Authorship Attribution of Females

In attributing the authorship of the 23 female authors, the sentiment and keyword feature set outperformed the lexico-syntactic feature set. Furthermore, the combined strength of these two feature sets surpassed their individual strengths.

According to the attribution results of the lexico-syntactic feature set for the females (see Table 15), all of the seven eigenvalues suggested weak discriminant functions (eigenvalue < 1). The results of Wilks's lambda indicated that five of the seven functions were significant (p < .05). Overall, both the original and cross-validated accuracy rates provided statistically significant evidence of the

Table 12 Attribution results of lexico-syntactic feature set for older males

Number of authors	Number of predictors	Functions	Eigenvalue	Wilks' lambda	Sig. of function	OAR (%)	CVAR (%)
6	7	Function 1	5.116	.040	.000	77.8	71.1
		Function 2	1.164	.247	.000		
		Function 3	.506	.535	.000		
		Function 4	.143	.806	.023		
		Function 5	.085	.921	.080		

Note: Sig. = significance; OAR = original accuracy rate; CVAR = cross-validated accuracy rate.

Table 13 Attribution results of sentiment and keyword feature set for older males

Number of authors	Number of predictors	Functions	Eigenvalue	Wilks' lambda	Sig. of function	OAR (%)	CVAR (%)
6	7	Function 1	1.236	.151	.000	65.6	57.8
		Function 2	.774	.338	.000		
		Function 3	.460	.599	.000		
		Function 4	.093	.875	.202		
		Function 5	.045	.957	.305		

Note: Sig. = significance; OAR = original accuracy rate; CVAR = cross-validated accuracy rate.

Table 14 Attribution results of combined feature set for older males

Number of authors	Number of predictors	Functions	Eigenvalue	Wilks' lambda	Sig. of function	OAR (%)	CVAR (%)
6	14	Function 1	6.408	.008	.000	90.0	83.3
		Function 2	2.243	.062	.000		
		Function 3	1.158	.202	.000		
		Function 4	.768	.436	.000		
		Function 5	.298	.770	.024		

Note: Sig. = significance; OAR = original accuracy rate; CVAR = cross-validated accuracy rate.

Table 15 Attribution results of lexico-syntactic feature set for females

Number of authors	Number of predictors	Functions	Eigenvalue	Wilks' lambda	Sig. of function	OAR (%)	CVAR (%)
23	7	Function 1	.935	.139	.000	25.7	19.3
		Function 2	.866	.268	.000		
		Function 3	.307	.501	.000		
		Function 4	.218	.654	.000		
		Function 5	.133	.797	.036		
		Function 6	.072	.903	.503		
		Function 7	.033	.968	.826		

Note: Sig. = significance; OAR = original accuracy rate; CVAR = cross-validated accuracy rate.

model's ability to predict outcomes, exceeding the proportional by-chance accuracy rate, which is 5.4% (100%/23*1.25).

According to the attribution results of sentiment and keyword feature set for the females (Table 16), all of the seven eigenvalues suggested weak discriminant functions (eigenvalue < 1). The results of Wilks's lambda showed that five of the seven functions were significant ($p < .05$). Overall, both the original and the cross-validated accuracy rates provided statistically significant evidence of the model's ability to predict outcomes, exceeding the proportional by-chance accuracy rate of 5.4% (100%/23*1.25).

The results of the combined feature set (see Table 17) show that 2 of the 14 eigenvalues indicated strong discriminant functions (eigenvalue > 1). Wilks's lambda results indicated that 7 of the 14 functions were significant ($p < .05$). Accordingly, both the original and cross-validated accuracy rates provided statistically significant evidence of the model's ability to predict outcomes, significantly exceeding the proportional by-chance accuracy rate, which is 5.4% (100%/23*1.25).

Based on these results, it is obvious that in the attribution of the 23 female authors, the sentiment and keyword feature set performed better than the lexico-syntactic feature set. In addition, the combined feature set outperformed the individual feature sets, which suggested that both feature sets were making positive contributions to the attribution of the 23 female authors. In addition, the combined strength of the two feature sets seemed to surpass the sum of the strengths of each individual group in terms of the number of larger eigenvalues.

Sentiment Scores and Keywords in the Authorship Attribution of Males

In attributing the authorship of the 12 male authors, the lexico-syntactic feature set outperformed the sentiment and keyword feature set. Furthermore, the combined strength of these two feature sets outperformed their individual strengths.

According to the attribution results of the lexico-syntactic feature set for the males (see Table 18), two of the seven eigenvalues indicated strong discriminant functions (eigenvalue > 1). The results of Wilks's lambda indicated that five of the seven functions were significant ($p < .05$). Accordingly, both the original and cross-validated accuracy rates provided statistically significant evidence of the model's ability to predict outcomes, significantly surpassing the proportional by-chance accuracy rate of 10.4% (100%/12*1.25).

According to the attribution results of sentiment and keyword feature set for the males (Table 19), one of the seven eigenvalues suggested a strong discriminant function (eigenvalue > 1). The results of Wilks's lambda showed that five

Table 16 Attribution results of sentiment and keyword feature set for females

Number of authors	Number of predictors	Functions	Eigenvalue	Wilks' lambda	Sig. of function	OAR (%)	CVAR (%)
23	7	Function 1	.637	.204	.000	29.8	22.8
		Function 2	.400	.334	.000		
		Function 3	.277	.468	.000		
		Function 4	.242	.598	.000		
		Function 5	.179	.742	.000		
		Function 6	.109	.874	.122		
		Function 7	.031	.970	.865		

Note: Sig. = significance; OAR = original accuracy rate; CVAR = cross-validated accuracy rate.

Table 17 Attribution results of combined feature set for females

Number of authors	Number of predictors	Functions	Eigenvalue	Wilks' lambda	Sig. of function	OAR (%)	CVAR (%)
23	14	Function 1	1.158	.034	.000	39.2	28.4
		Function 2	1.085	.073	.000		
		Function 3	.687	.151	.000		
		Function 4	.376	.255	.000		
		Function 5	.291	.351	.000		
		Function 6	.234	.454	.000		
		Function 7	.219	.56	.001		
		Function 8	.141	.683	.109		
		Function 9	.092	.779	.588		
		Function 10	.053	.850	.873		
		Function 11	.049	.896	.908		
		Function 12	.037	.940	.963		
		Function 13	.015	.974	.988		
		Function 14	.011	.989	.939		

Note: Sig. = significance; OAR = original accuracy rate; CVAR = cross-validated accuracy rate.

Table 18 Attribution results of lexico-syntactic feature set for males

Number of authors	Number of predictors	Functions	Eigenvalue	Wilks' lambda	Sig. of function	OAR (%)	CVAR (%)
12	7	Function 1	6.385	.018	.000	62.6	55.3
		Function 2	2.091	.135	.000		
		Function 3	.675	.418	.000		
		Function 4	.159	.700	.002		
		Function 5	.135	.811	.027		
		Function 6	.074	.921	.310		
		Function 7	.011	.989	.878		

Note Sig. = significance; OAR = original accuracy rate; CVAR = cross-validated accuracy rate.

Table 19 Attribution results of sentiment and keyword feature set for males

Number of authors	Number of predictors	Functions	Eigenvalue	Wilks' lambda	Sig. of function	OAR (%)	CVAR (%)
12	7	Function 1	2.288	.061	.000	58.7	46.9
		Function 2	.777	.199	.000		
		Function 3	.569	.354	.000		
		Function 4	.325	.555	.000		
		Function 5	.201	.736	.000		
		Function 6	.100	.884	.053		
		Function 7	.029	.972	.438		

Note: Sig. = significance; OAR = original accuracy rate; CVAR = cross-validated accuracy rate.

of the seven functions were significant ($p < .05$). Accordingly, both the original and the cross-validated accuracy rates provided statistically significant evidence of the model's ability to predict outcomes, significantly exceeding the proportional by-chance accuracy rate of 10.4% (100%/12*1.25).

The results of the combined feature set (see Table 20) show that four of the 11 eigenvalues suggested very strong discriminant functions (eigenvalue > 1). Wilks's lambda results indicated that eight of the 11 functions were significant ($p < .05$). Accordingly, both the original and cross-validated accuracy rates provided statistically significant evidence of the model's ability to predict outcomes, considerably exceeding the proportional by-chance accuracy rate, which stands at 10.4% (100%/12*1.25).

Based on the preceding results, it is clear that in the attribution of the 12 male authors, the lexico-syntactic feature set outperformed the sentiment and keyword feature set. In addition, the combined feature set outperformed the individual feature sets, which suggested that both feature sets were making their positive contributions to the attribution of the 12 male authors. In addition, the combined strength of the two feature sets seemed to surpass the sum of the strengths of each individual group in terms of the number of larger eigenvalues.

Sentiment Scores and Keywords in the Authorship Attribution of Younger Authors

In the task of attributing the 24 younger authors, the sentiment and keyword feature set outperformed the lexico-syntactic feature set. Further, the combined strength of these two feature sets also surpassed their individual performances.

According to the attribution results of the lexico-syntactic feature set for the younger authors (see Table 21), one of the seven eigenvalues suggested a strong discriminant function (eigenvalue > 1). The results of Wilks's lambda revealed that four of the seven functions were significant ($p < .05$). Accordingly, both the original and cross-validated accuracy rates provided statistically significant evidence of the model's ability to predict outcomes. These rates significantly exceeded the proportional by-chance accuracy rate of 5.2% (100%/24*1.25).

According to the attribution results of sentiment and keyword feature set for the younger authors (see Table 22), all of the seven eigenvalues indicated weak discriminant functions (eigenvalue < 1). The results of Wilks's lambda indicated that five of the seven functions were significant ($p < .05$). Overall, both the original and the cross-validated accuracy rates provided statistically significant evidence of the model's ability to predict outcomes. These rates significantly exceeded the proportional by-chance accuracy rate of 5.2% (100%/24*1.25).

Table 20 Attribution results of combined feature set for males

Number of authors	Number of predictors	Functions	Eigenvalue	Wilks' lambda	Sig. of function	OAR (%)	CVAR (%)
12	14	Function 1	6.598	.002	.000	83.2	70.9
		Function 2	2.441	.014	.000		
		Function 3	2.014	.048	.000		
		Function 4	1.085	.144	.000		
		Function 5	.571	.300	.000		
		Function 6	.295	.471	.000		
		Function 7	.200	.61	.000		
		Function 8	.180	.732	.004		
		Function 9	.079	.863	.146		
		Function 10	.047	.931	.300		
		Function 11	.026	.975	.381		

Note: Sig. = significance; OAR = original accuracy rate; CVAR = cross-validated accuracy rate.

Table 21 Attribution results of lexico-syntactic feature set for younger authors

Number of authors	Number of predictors	Functions	Eigenvalue	Wilks' lambda	Sig. of function	OAR (%)	CVAR (%)
24	7	Function 1	1.670	.079	.000	31.9	25.3
		Function 2	.842	.212	.000		
		Function 3	.489	.39	.000		
		Function 4	.313	.581	.000		
		Function 5	.171	.763	.002		
		Function 6	.076	.894	.353		
		Function 7	.039	.962	.716		

Note: Sig. = significance; OAR = original accuracy rate; CVAR = cross-validated accuracy rate.

Table 22 Attribution results of sentiment and keyword feature set for younger authors

Number of authors	Number of predictors	Functions	Eigenvalue	Wilks' lambda	Sig. of function	OAR (%)	CVAR (%)
24	7	Function 1	.988	.115	.000	36.1	25.6
		Function 2	.902	.228	.000		
		Function 3	.358	.433	.000		
		Function 4	.230	.588	.000		
		Function 5	.200	.723	.000		
		Function 6	.109	.868	.077		
		Function 7	.039	.962	.719		

Note: Sig. = significance; OAR = original accuracy rate; CVAR = cross-validated accuracy rate.

Table 23 Attribution results of combined feature set for younger authors

Number of authors	Number of predictors	Functions	Eigenvalue	Wilks' lambda	Sig. of function	OAR (%)	CVAR (%)
24	14	Function 1	1.951	.012	.000	50.6	38.1
		Function 2	1.330	.036	.000		
		Function 3	.797	.083	.000		
		Function 4	.704	.149	.000		
		Function 5	.503	.254	.000		
		Function 6	.270	.382	.000		
		Function 7	.230	.486	.000		
		Function 8	.192	.597	.000		
		Function 9	.170	.712	.036		
		Function 10	.067	.833	.733		
		Function 11	.051	.888	.883		
		Function 12	.034a	.933	.947		
		Function 13	.023a	.965	.954		
		Function 14	.013a	.987	.922		

Note: Sig. = significance; OAR = original accuracy rate; CVAR = cross-validated accuracy rate.

The results of the combined feature set (see Table 23) showed that 2 of the 14 eigenvalues indicated strong discriminant functions (eigenvalue > 1). Wilks's lambda results indicated that nine of the 14 functions were significant ($p < .05$). Accordingly, both the original and cross-validated accuracy rates provided statistically significant evidence of the model's ability to predict outcomes, significantly exceeding the proportional by-chance accuracy rate of 5.2% (100%/24*1.25).

Based on these results, it is clear that in attributing the 24 younger authors, the sentiment and keyword feature set performed better than the lexico-syntactic feature set. In addition, the combined feature set outperformed the individual feature sets, suggesting that both feature sets positively contributed to the attribution of the 24 younger authors. Furthermore, the combined strength of the two feature sets seemed to surpass the sum of the strengths of each individual group in terms of the number of larger eigenvalues.

Sentiment Scores and Keywords in the Authorship Attribution of Older Authors

In the task of attributing the 11 older authors, the lexico-syntactic feature set outperformed the sentiment and keyword feature set. Furthermore, the combined strength of these two feature sets also surpassed their individual performances.

According to the attribution results of the lexico-syntactic feature set for the older authors (see Table 24), one of the seven eigenvalues suggested a strong discriminant function (eigenvalue > 1). The results of Wilks's lambda revealed that four of the seven functions were significant ($p < .05$). Accordingly, both the original and cross-validated accuracy rates provided statistically significant evidence of the model's ability to predict outcomes. These rates significantly exceeded the proportional by-chance accuracy rate of 11.4% (100%/11*1.25).

According to the attribution results of sentiment and keyword feature set for the older authors (see Table 25), all of the seven eigenvalues suggested weak discriminant functions (eigenvalue < 1). The results of Wilks's lambda showed that four of the seven functions were significant ($p < .05$). Overall, both the original and the cross-validated accuracy rates provided statistically significant evidence of the model's ability to predict outcomes. These rates significantly exceed the proportional by-chance accuracy rate of 11.4% (100%/11*1.25).

The results of the combined feature set (see Table 26) showed that two of the ten eigenvalues indicated strong discriminant functions (eigenvalue > 1). Wilks's lambda results indicated that six of the ten functions were significant

Table 24 Attribution results of lexico-syntactic feature set for older authors

Number of authors	Number of predictors	Functions	Eigenvalue	Wilks' lambda	Sig. of function	OAR (%)	CVAR (%)
11	7	Function 1	2.339	.081	.000	54.9	45.7
		Function 2	.934	.272	.000		
		Function 3	.370	.526	.000		
		Function 4	.155	.721	.007		
		Function 5	.118	.833	.065		
		Function 6	.037	.931	.368		
		Function 7	.035	.966	.260		

Note: Sig. = significance; OAR = original accuracy rate; CVAR = cross-validated accuracy rate.

Table 25 Attribution results of sentiment and keyword feature set for older authors

Number of authors	Number of predictors	Functions	Eigenvalue	Wilks' lambda	Sig. of function	OAR (%)	CVAR (%)
11	7	Function 1	.882	.184	.000	48.1	36.4
		Function 2	.433	.347	.000		
		Function 3	.394	.498	.000		
		Function 4	.209	.693	.001		
		Function 5	.104	.838	.082		
		Function 6	.069	.925	.301		
		Function 7	.011	.990	.810		

Note: Sig. = significance; OAR = original accuracy rate; CVAR = cross-validated accuracy rate.

Table 26 Attribution results of combined feature set for older authors

Number of authors	Number of predictors	Functions	Eigenvalue	Wilks' lambda	Sig. of function	OAR (%)	CVAR (%)
11	14	Function 1	2.776	.020	.000	74.7	58.0
		Function 2	1.269	.076	.000		
		Function 3	.717	.173	.000		
		Function 4	.522	.297	.000		
		Function 5	.300	.451	.000		
		Function 6	.271	.587	.001		
		Function 7	.174	.745	.082		
		Function 8	.099	.875	.530		
		Function 9	.035	.962	.926		
		Function 10	.004	.996	.987		

Note: Sig. = significance; OAR = original accuracy rate; CVAR = cross-validated accuracy rate.

($p < .05$). Accordingly, both the original and cross-validated accuracy rates provided statistically significant evidence of the model's ability to predict outcomes, significantly exceeding the proportional by-chance accuracy rate of 11.4% (100%/11*1.25).

Based on these results, it is clear that in attributing the 11 older authors, the lexico-syntactic feature set outperformed the sentiment and keyword feature set. Moreover, the combined feature set outperformed the individual feature sets, suggesting that both feature sets were making their positive contributions to the attribution of the 11 older authors. In addition, the combined strength of the two feature sets seemed to surpass the sum of the strengths of each individual group in terms of the number of larger eigenvalues.

Sentiment Scores and Keywords in the Authorship Attribution of All Authors

In the attribution of all of the 35 authors, the sentiment and keyword feature set outperformed the lexico-syntactic feature set. Furthermore, the combined strength of these two feature sets also surpassed their individual performances.

According to the attribution results of the lexico-syntactic feature set for all of the authors (see Table 27), one of the seven eigenvalues suggested a strong discriminant function (eigenvalue > 1). The results of Wilks's lambda revealed that five of the seven functions were significant ($p < .05$). Accordingly, both the original and cross-validated accuracy rates provided statistically significant evidence of the model's ability to predict outcomes. These rates significantly exceeded the proportional by-chance accuracy rate of 3.6% (100%/35*1.25).

According to the attribution results of sentiment and keyword feature set for all of the authors (see Table 28), all of the seven eigenvalues suggested weak discriminant functions (eigenvalue < 1). The results of Wilks's lambda indicated that all of the seven functions were significant ($p < .05$). Overall, both the original and the cross-validated accuracy rates provided statistically significant evidence of the model's ability to predict outcomes, exceeding the proportional by-chance accuracy rate of 3.6% (100%/35*1.25).

The results of the combined feature set (see Table 29) showed that 2 of the 14 eigenvalues suggested strong discriminant functions (eigenvalue > 1). Wilks's lambda results indicated that 10 of the 14 functions were significant ($p < .05$). Accordingly, both the original and cross-validated accuracy rates provided statistically significant evidence of the model's ability to predict outcomes, significantly exceeding the proportional by-chance accuracy rate, which is 3.6% (100%/35*1.25).

Table 27 Attribution results of lexico-syntactic feature set for all authors

Number of authors	Number of predictors	Functions	Eigenvalue	Wilks' lambda	Sig. of function	OAR (%)	CVAR (%)
35	7	Function 1	1.775	.080	.000	25.1	19.7
		Function 2	.874	.222	.000		
		Function 3	.406	.416	.000		
		Function 4	.275	.585	.000		
		Function 5	.174	.745	.000		
		Function 6	.081	.875	.201		
		Function 7	.057	.946	.480		

Note: Sig. = significance; OAR = original accuracy rate; CVAR = cross-validated accuracy rate.

Table 28 Attribution results of sentiment and keyword feature set for all authors

Number of authors	Number of predictors	Functions	Eigenvalue	Wilks' lambda	Sig. of function	OAR (%)	CVAR (%)
35	7	Function 1	.841	.132	.000	28.0	21.1
		Function 2	.622	.242	.000		
		Function 3	.353	.393	.000		
		Function 4	.235	.532	.000		
		Function 5	.196	.657	.000		
		Function 6	.160	.786	.000		
		Function 7	.097	.911	.016		

Note: Sig. = significance; OAR = original accuracy rate; CVAR = cross-validated accuracy rate.

Table 29 Attribution results of combined feature set for all authors

Number of authors	Number of predictors	Functions	Eigenvalue	Wilks' lambda	Sig. of function	OAR (%)	CVAR (%)
35	14	Function 1	1.901	.013	.000	42.7	34.3
		Function 2	1.042	.037	.000		
		Function 3	.824	.075	.000		
		Function 4	.618	.136	.000		
		Function 5	.436	.22	.000		
		Function 6	.304	.317	.000		
		Function 7	.227	0413	.000		
		Function 8	.183	.506	.000		
		Function 9	.176	.599	.000		
		Function 10	.158	.704	.003		
		Function 11	.081	.815	.336		
		Function 12	.067	.881	.688		
		Function 13	.040	.941	.941		
		Function 14	.022	.978	.966		

Note: Sig. = significance; OAR = original accuracy rate; CVAR = cross-validated accuracy rate.

Based on these results, it is obvious that in the attribution of the 35 authors, the sentiment and keyword feature set outperformed the lexico-syntactic feature set. Moreover, the combined feature set outperformed the individual feature set, suggesting that both feature sets positively contributed to the attribution of the 35 authors. In addition, the combined strength of the two feature sets seemed to surpass the sum of the strengths of each individual group in terms of the number of larger eigenvalues.

3.2.2 Summary for Authorship Attribution

Based on the attribution results, two key points emerged. Firstly, the distinctive profiling features, including sentiment and keyword features, were also effective in authorship attribution tasks, even when compared to the well-established lexico-syntactic feature set. Secondly, more accurately, these profiling features outperformed the lexico-syntactic in four out of the nine attribution tests. These tests targeted younger female authors, all female authors, all younger authors, and a collective group of all 35 authors. Notably, each group contained younger female authors, which signifies a commonality among them.

This finding suggests that the distinctive profiling features have a greater sensitivity towards younger females' texts than the lexico-syntactic features. This sensitivity is closely associated with the profiling strength of these features. More specifically, the profiling features are distinctive among different gender and age groups, indicating the sensitivity of specific gender and age groups towards the features. In addition, the sentiment and keyword features are presumed to exhibit greater diversity among younger female authors than the lexico-syntactic features. This assumption is partly corroborated by the finding of sentiment scores in profiling gender groups and age groups in private texts, in which the sentiment scores of the younger authors ($SD = 90.51$) and the female authors ($SD = 73.53$) display greater diversity than those of the older authors ($SD = 69.90$) and the male authors ($SD = 54.03$), respectively.

This variation in sentiment scores may partially explain why the entire sentiment and keyword feature set is more sensitive and distinctive when this gender-and-age-related group of younger females is involved. However, it is also important to note that this diversity is not sufficient to confuse different gender or age identities, thereby aligning with the results of the profiling experiment where sentiment scores were a distinctive feature for profiling or predicting the gender of text authors.

These findings are consistent with the notion that younger people and females are generally more emotionally unstable and experience more mood swings than older people and males. Specifically, women's bodies produce less testosterone (Shakouri et al., 2015), and more estrogen than men's bodies, which might accordingly render female authors emotionally less stable (Albert & Newhouse, 2019) than their male counterparts. Furthermore, older people are often perceived to become more emotionally stable as they age (Pennebaker, 2011a), potentially due to increased life experience, improved coping skills, and hormone changes leading to emotional stability. This underscores the possible influence of hormones on age-related differences in language usage.

3.3 Research Question 3: Authorship and Mindset

Authorship is a complex and multifaceted concept encompassing a myriad of different aspects. It is shaped profoundly by our cognitive filter, or more precisely, our mindset (Earley et al., 2007; Gupta & Govindarajan, 2002; Sistek-Chandler, 2019). The results of this study indicate that the development of authorship is influenced by our mindset, which involves both inherent hormonal factors (Berenbaum & Beltz, 2016; Einstein et al., 2013; Kiyar et al., 2022; Pennebaker, 2011a; Shakouri et al., 2015) and external social factors (Gupta & Govindarajan, 2002).

On the one hand, the inherent factors refer to an individual's innate predisposition to writing, influenced notably by genetics, particularly hormones (Berenbaum & Beltz, 2016; Einstein et al., 2013; Kiyar et al., 2022; Pennebaker, 2011a). According to the results of the sentiment scores, female authors tend to express more negative emotions than their male counterparts in private texts, revealing more about their authentic selves. Public texts, especially professional public texts, are typically crafted for a specific audience or the public. These public texts strive to deliver information or a message succinctly and clearly. Consequently, they undergo greater scrutiny and editing than private texts.

These findings align with the previous research suggesting that females tend to report experiencing more negative emotions than males, presumably due to their exhibited stronger reactions to unpleasant events (Fiorentini, 2013; Kring & Gordon, 1998). This propensity seems to be closely related to another observation from the study: female and younger authors are more likely to use personal pronouns and graduations in their texts than male and older authors. The close connection is further supported by the notion that the use of pronouns reflects a person's focus of attention: depressive emotions could correlate with higher pronoun use, particularly first-person singular pronouns such as 'I', 'me', and 'my' (Pennebaker, 2011a; Pennebaker, 2011b).

The frequent use of graduations, such as intensifiers, is often associated with strong emotional expressions, which are also indicators and hallmarks of female authorship (Pennebaker, 2011a). Further, this is also consistent with an empirical study about the relationship between testosterone injection and language use (Pennebaker, 2011a), which found that the dropping of testosterone correlated with the increased use of social pronouns such as 'he', 'she', 'we', and 'they'.

On the other hand, social factors also play a significant role in shaping an individual's development as an author. Based on the results of this study, the fluctuations of the sentiment scores in the four authors' texts have been confirmed to be linked closely to the emotional tumults stemming from various life experiences.

In conclusion, while inherent factors may define an individual's natural propensity for writing, external social factors can also influence the development of authorship. Collectively, they shape an individual's mindset.

3.3.1 Interplay between Authorship Profiling and Attribution

A foundational underlying link between authorship profiling and authorship attribution has been substantiated in the current study, predicated on the shared use of the distinctive authorship profiling features in the tasks of authorship attribution. Authorship is inextricably intertwined with an author's mindset. Therefore, analysing authorship from different perspectives or purposes might result in different tasks. Nevertheless, these tasks should be interconnected (Deutsch & Paraboni, 2022) due to a foundational link, namely, authorship.

Moreover, the performance of these shared features exhibits certain characteristics directly related to their profiling strength. Specifically, the profiling features tested in this study proved to be distinctive in distinguishing both gender and age, with heightened sensitivity to younger female authors in the attribution tasks. In other words, these features performed more efficiently in the attribution tasks involving this particular gender-and-age-related group. As mentioned in Section 3.2.2, this could partly be ascribed to the greater diversity of the sentiment scores in both the younger and female groups, which was observed in the profiling experiment. Such a correlation facilitates the sharing of features between authorship profiling and authorship attribution tasks.

3.3.2 Interplay among Gender, Authorship, and Mindset

The profiling results of sentiment analysis and keyness analysis suggest a hidden gender-related link between the sentiment scores and the use of pronouns and graduations, Specifically, female authors tend to write more pessimistic and emotionally volatile texts and are inclined to use personal pronouns more frequently than male authors.

More specifically, the female authors consistently exhibit significantly lower sentiment scores than the male authors in their private texts, where they may feel liberated to express their true selves. This suggests that female authors exhibit more pessimism in their writings than male authors. This pessimism in the female writings seems to be consistently correlated with their more frequent use of personal pronouns (Newman et al., 2008; Pennebaker, 2011a; Pennebaker, 2011b; Pennebaker & Stone, 2003; Rude et al., 2004; Tausczik & Pennebaker, 2010) and graduations.

In addition, there is a noticeable trend that female authors tend to have higher standard deviations (SD = 73.53 in private texts and SD = 60.71 in public texts) in their sentiment scores than male authors (SD = 54.03 in private texts and SD = 52.50 in public texts). This trend might suggest that females are emotionally less stable than males (Pennebaker, 2011a; Pennebaker, 2011b). Combined, these results indicate that pessimistic females are emotionally less stable and use personal pronouns significantly more frequently in speaking or writing than optimistic and emotionally stable males (Pennebaker, 2011a; Pennebaker, 2011b).

Particularly, these associations resonate with prior research findings that the frequent use of personal pronouns, especially the first-person singular pronouns, correlates with depressive emotions, even linking to higher levels of depression and suicide rates (Newman et al., 2008; Pennebaker, 2011a; Pennebaker, 2011b; Pennebaker & Stone, 2003; Rude et al., 2004; Tausczik & Pennebaker, 2010). Therefore, the connection between female authors' more pessimistic and emotionally unstable writings, and their propensity for using personal pronouns is confirmed and substantiated. In summary, female authors who write more pessimistic and emotionally unstable texts tend to use personal pronouns more frequently.

The correlation between females being more pessimistic and emotionally unstable and their higher likelihood of using graduations seemed to be indirect and less substantiated. More graduations may entail the more frequent use of intensive adverbs to indicate the degree or intensity of a particular evaluative category (Newman et al., 2008). Such intensive adverbs may be linked with the intensity of various emotions and mood swings. Specifically, the frequent use of graduations, especially intensifiers, may signify a higher degree of emotional instability and intensity. For instance, an individual frequently using the term 'very' to express emotions might indicate experiencing more severe mood swings and heightened emotional intensity than someone who does not use such intensifiers as frequently. This pattern could be related to factors like personality traits, hormonal fluctuations, and life experiences. Further exploration into this relationship would be valuable. Meanwhile, the correlation between female authors' more pessimistic writings and their increased usage of graduations is not convincingly established.

Collectively, such tendencies may partly be attributed to different hormonal levels between females and males (Berenbaum & Beltz, 2016; Einstein et al., 2013; Kiyar et al., 2022; Pennebaker, 2011a). These hormonal disparities may potentially manifest as differences in emotional responses. Specifically, women's bodies produce much less testosterone (Shakouri et al., 2015) and more estrogen than men's, which render female authors less optimistic and emotionally less stable (Albert & Newhouse, 2019) than the male authors.

3.3.3 Interplay between Age and Gender

Remarkably, the results of this study also indicate a similarity in the language use tendencies between the younger and female authors.

As for the sentiment scores, the female authors (M = 37.08) consistently demonstrate significantly lower scores than the male authors (M = 94.02) in the private texts (p = .012). Even though the sentiment score differences between the younger and older authors are not significant in the private texts (p = .07), it is evident that younger authors (M = 55.72) expressed less positivity in their writings than older authors (M = 92.10).

With respect to the function keywords, both personal pronouns (p < .001) and graduations (p = .002) can significantly predict authors' gender. Specifically, female authors are six times more likely to use personal pronouns than male authors (OR = 6.387) and three times more likely to use graduations than male authors (OR = 2.907). In the same vein, the differences in the usage of personal pronouns (p = .008) and graduations (p = .011) can significantly predict author gender between younger and older authors in the use of personal pronouns and graduations were significantly established. Both personal pronouns (p = .008) and graduations (p = .011) can significantly predict author gender. Specifically, younger authors were three times more likely to use personal pronouns than older ones (OR = 3.288) and nearly three times more likely to use graduations than older ones (OR = 2.59).

Furthermore, as discussed in Section 3.1.2, there is a clear trend in both private and public writings showing that the younger authors (SD = 90.51 in private texts and SD = 63.76 in public texts) and the female authors (SD = 73.53 in private texts and SD = 60.71 in public texts) tend to have higher standard deviations in their sentiment scores than older ones (SD = 69.90 in private texts and SD = 50.20 in public texts) and male authors (SD = 54.03 in private texts and SD = 52.50 in public texts), respectively. This signifies that the variation or diversity within the sentiment scores of younger and female authors is much greater than that of older and male authors, suggesting more severe mood swings in both younger and female authors.

Mood swings can be more common or more severe in females than males, particularly during certain life stages such as puberty, menstruation, pregnancy, and menopause. As mentioned earlier, inherent hormonal fluctuations may contribute to these mood swings (Shakouri et al., 2015), and other external social factors such as stress, lifestyle changes, and social support. Similarly, younger authors may experience more frequent or intense mood swings due to factors such as hormonal changes and a lack of experience in managing personal emotions. This contrasts with older authors who may have greater emotional stability due to a decline in certain hormones, such as testosterone (Shakouri et al., 2015), and more emotional management experience (Pennebaker, 2011a).

Taken together, these findings suggest that the tendencies for female authors and younger authors to be more negative and more emotionally unstable are closely associated with a higher likelihood of using the depression indicators, such as first-person singular pronouns, and the mood swing indicators, such as graduations.

Overall, these findings are consistent perfectly with earlier interesting observations about the language of gender and age that 'older people often use function words like men and younger people tend to use them like women' (Pennebaker, 2011a, p. 56) and that depressed people tend to use first-person singular pronoun more often than emotionally stable people (Pennebaker, 2011b). More interestingly, Pennebaker (2011a) also noted that such similar tendencies or patterns between the writings of younger authors and female authors 'hold up across cultures, languages and centuries' (Pennebaker, 2011a, p. 56), a notion which is confirmed and supported by this study.

4 Conclusion

Major Findings

This study contributes to the understanding of authorship by testing and confirming the distinctiveness of the sentiment scores, personal pronouns, and graduations in profiling and attributing authors in the Chinese cultural context. In this study, a foundational underlying link between authorship profiling and authorship attribution has been established based on a series of feature tests for authors from various demographic backgrounds. Besides, the consistent yet gradual changeability of gender-related and age-related authorship has been acknowledged. This variability occurs throughout an author's life under the influence of individual mindset. Specifically, three major findings corresponding to the three research questions have been highlighted.

Firstly, significant differences in sentiment scores and keywords exist with respect to authors' gender, age, and text genre (authorship profiling). To be accurate, it is found that 1) the sentiment scores are relatively consistent and stable within authors; 2) male authors display significantly more positive sentiment scores in their private writings than female authors, indicating greater optimism among males in private writings; 3) keywords, especially the personal pronouns and graduations, are distinctive in predicting authors' gender and age. More specifically, female authors and younger authors are more likely to use personal pronouns and graduations than male authors and older authors, respectively. Furthermore, male authors show conspicuously the highest sentiment scores in Online Chats, which is one type of the private writings. This might be indicative of a high degree of optimism in social interactive communications.

Secondly, the distinctive profiling features, including sentiment and keyword features, are also effective in authorship attribution tasks compared to the well-established lexico-syntactic feature set. These profiling features outperform the lexico-syntactic in four of the nine attribution tests, which include tests for younger females, all females, all younger authors, and all 35 authors. This indicates that the distinctive profiling features are more sensitive to certain demographic factors of authors than lexico-syntactic features, likely due to the profiling strength of these features.

Thirdly, authorship is shaped by our cognitive filter, namely, mindset which is influenced by both our innate hormones and external social experiences. More specifically, gender-related mindset has been more strongly confirmed and supported than age-related mindset. Moreover, similar patterns of language use in both younger authors and female authors have been identified and provisionally interpreted.

Contributions

Therefore, these findings contribute to authorship analysis both theoretically and practically by addressing how the sentiment and keyword features correlated with authorship through the lens of mindset.

Theoretically, the findings broaden the scope of authorship features, venturing into previously underexplored domains like sentiment analysis and keyness analysis. This expansion establishes a foundational link between authorship profiling and authorship attribution tasks. Specifically, the findings suggest that the consistent usage of sentiment expressions and certain keywords, namely, personal pronouns and graduations, may constitute an integral part of authorship style, thereby rendering them reliable linguistic feature candidates for both authorship profiling and authorship attribution tasks.

In addition, the concept of mindset has been both substantiated and extended in relation to authorship. Specifically, the patterns of gender and age differences in private writings in terms of the sentiment scores and function keywords, have been identified and explained using the mindset paradigm. This exploration has also shed light on the interplay between age and gender in these patterns.

Practically, the findings offer some rough quantitative references for the practice of authorship profiling.

1) On the one hand, in private writings, the sentiment scores ranging from −70 or lower to +59 are typically indicative of female authors. On the other hand, the sentiment scores ranging from +70 to +307 or higher suggest male authors. In public writings, the sentiment scores depend largely on the topics of the writings. Besides, in interactive communications with peers, higher scores ranging from 122 to 370 or higher are indicative of male authors.

2) In terms of the function keywords, male authors are nearly ten times more likely to avoid using personal pronouns ($OR = 9.828$) than to use them and five times more likely to avoid using graduations ($OR = 5.09$) than to use them. Similarly, older authors are almost five times more likely to avoid using personal pronouns ($OR = 4.673$) and three times more likely to avoid using graduations ($OR = 3.142$). In more detail, female authors are six times more likely to use personal pronouns than male authors ($OR = 6.387$) and three times more likely to use graduations than male authors ($OR = 2.907$). Younger authors are three times more likely to use personal pronouns than the older authors ($OR = 3.288$) and nearly three times more likely to use graduations than the older authors ($OR = 2.59$). These tentative benchmarks could prove valuable for forensic linguists in real-world authorship analysis cases.

Future Research Direction

In this study, keyword features are based on the linguistic tendencies of female authors. However, male authors are also claimed to have some distinctive linguistic tendencies, such as using more articles, nouns, and prepositions, since they tend to be more informative (Newman et al., 2008; Pennebaker, 2011a) in communication. These gender tendencies warrant further exploration in both authorship profiling and authorship attribution in future research.

References

Ainsworth, J., & Juola, P. (2018). Who wrote this: Modern forensic authorship analysis as a model for valid forensic science. *Washington University Law Review, 96*, 1159.

Albahli, S. (2022). Twitter sentiment analysis: An Arabic text mining approach based on COVID-19. *Frontiers in Public Health, 10*, 1–13.

Albert, K. M., & Newhouse, P. A. (2019). Estrogen, stress, and depression: Cognitive and biological interactions. *Annual Review of Clinical Psychology, 15*, 399–423.

Berenbaum, S. A., & Beltz, A. M. (2016). How early hormones shape gender development. *Current Opinion in Behavioral Sciences, 7*, 53–60. DOI: https://doi.org/10.1016/j.cobeha.2015.11.011.

Bevendorff, J., Chulvi, B., De La Peña Sarracén, G. L. et al. (2021). Overview of PAN 2021: Authorship verification, profiling hate speech spreaders on Twitter, and style change detection. In *Experimental IR Meets Multilinguality, Multimodality, and Interaction: 12th International Conference of the CLEF Association, CLEF 2021, Virtual Event, September 21–24, 2021, Proceedings 12* (pp. 567–73). Berlin: Springer International Publishing.

Bevendorff, J., Chulvi, B., Fersini, E. et al. (2022). Overview of PAN 2022: Authorship verification, profiling irony and stereotype spreaders, style change detection, and trigger detection. In *Advances in Information Retrieval: 44th European Conference on IR Research, ECIR 2022, Stavanger, Norway, April 10–14, 2022, Proceedings, Part II* (pp. 331–8). Berlin: Springer International Publishing.

Bevendorff, J., Ghanem, B., Giachanou, A. et al. (2020). Overview of PAN 2020: Authorship verification, celebrity profiling, profiling fake news spreaders on Twitter, and style change detection. In *Experimental IR Meets Multilinguality, Multimodality, and Interaction: 11th International Conference of the CLEF Association, CLEF 2020, Thessaloniki, Greece, September 22–25, 2020, Proceedings 11* (pp. 372–83). Berlin: Springer International Publishing.

Bianchin, M., & Angrilli, A. (2012). Gender differences in emotional responses: A psychophysiological study. *Physiology & Behavior, 105*(4), 925–32.

Biber, D., Conrad, S., & Leech, G. (2002). *The Longman Student Grammar of Spoken and Written English*. Harlow: Longman.

Biber, D., Conrad, S., & Reppen, R. (1998). *Corpus Linguistics: Investigating Language Structure and Use*. Cambridge: Cambridge University Press.

Birjali, M., Kasri, M., & Beni-Hssane, A. (2021). A comprehensive survey on sentiment analysis: Approaches, challenges and trends. *Knowledge-Based Systems*, *226*, 107134.

Bondi, M. (2010). Perspectives on keywords and keyness. In M. Bondi & M. Scott (eds.), *Keyness in Texts* (pp. 1–20). Amsterdam: John Benjamins Publishing Company.

Bondi, M., & Scott, M. (2010). *Keyness in Texts*. Amsterdam: John Benjamins Publishing Company.

Bordet, L. (2015). The renewal of intensifiers and variations in language registers: A case-study of very, really, so and totally. In *Intensity, Intensification and Intensifying Modification across Languages*. HAL open science.

Burns, R. P., & Burns, R. (2008). *Business Research Methods and Statistics Using SPSS*. London: Sage.

Casavantes, M., López, R., & González-Gurrola, L. C. (2019). UACh at MEX-A3T 2019: Preliminary results on detecting aggressive tweets by adding author information via an unsupervised strategy. In *Proceedings of the Iberian Languages Evaluation Forum (IberLEF 2023)* (pp. 537–43). http://ceur-ws.org/Vol-2421/.

Cigic, D., & Bugarski, V. (2010). Personality traits and colour preferences. *Current Topics in Neurology, Psychiatry and Related Disciplines; Journal of Association of Serbian Neurologists*, *18*(4), 28–35.

Cunningham, K. T., & Haley, K. L. (2020). Measuring lexical diversity for discourse analysis in aphasia: Moving-average type–token ratio and word information measure. *Journal of Speech, Language, and Hearing Research*, *63*(3), 710–21.

Degol, J. L., Wang, M. T., Zhang, Y., & Allerton, J. (2018). Do growth mindsets in math benefit females? Identifying pathways between gender, mindset, and motivation. *Journal of Youth and Adolescence*, *47*(5), 976–90.

Deutsch, C., & Paraboni, I. (2022). Authorship attribution using author profiling classifiers. *Natural Language Engineering*, *29*(1), 110–37.

Earley, P. C., Murnieks, C., & Mosakowski, E. (2007). Cultural intelligence and the global mindset. In Javidan, M., Steers, R. M. and Hitt, M. A. (eds.), *The Global Mindset* (Vol. 19, pp. 75–103). Leeds: Emerald Group Publishing Limited.

Einstein, G., Downar, J., & Kennedy, S. (2013). Gender/sex differences in emotions. *Medicographia*, *35*(3), 271–80.

Ezaldeen, H., Misra, R., Bisoy, S. K., Alatrash, R., & Priyadarshini, R. (2022). A hybrid E-learning recommendation integrating adaptive profiling and sentiment analysis. *Journal of Web Semantics*, *72*(C), 100700.

Febi, A. R., Manu, M. K., Mohapatra, A. K., Praharaj, S. K., & Guddattu, V. (2021). Psychological stress and health-related quality of life among tuberculosis patients: A prospective cohort study. *ERJ Open Research, 7*(3), 00251–2021.

Fiorentini, C. (2013). Gender and emotion expression, experience, physiology and well being: A psychological perspective. In Latu, I., Schmidt Mast, M., & Kaiser, S. (eds.), *Gender and Emotion: An Interdisciplinary Perspective*, 15–42. Lausanne: Peter Lang.

French, P., & Harrison, P. (2007). Position Statement concerning use of impressionistic likelihood terms in forensic speaker comparison cases, with a foreword by Peter French & Philip Harrison. *International Journal of Speech, Language and the Law, 14*(1), 137–44.

Gabrielatos, C. (2018). Keyness analysis: Nature, metrics and techniques. In Taylor, C. & Marchi, A. (eds.), *Corpus Approaches to Discourse: A Critical Review* (pp. 225–58). Oxfordshire: Routledge.

Garrido-Espinosa, M. G., Rosales-Pérez, A., & López-Monroy, A. P. (2020). GRU with author profiling information to detect aggressiveness. In *Proceedings of the Iberian Languages Evaluation Forum (IberLEF 2023)* (pp. 246–51). https://ceur-ws.org/Vol-2664/.

Grant, T. (2007). Quantifying evidence in forensic authorship analysis. *International Journal of Speech, Language & the Law, 14*(1), 1–25.

Grant, T. (2013). TXT 4N6: Method, consistency, and distinctiveness in the analysis of SMS text messages. *Harvard Journal of Law & Public Policy, 21* (2), 467–94.

Grant, T. (2022). *The Idea of Progress in Forensic Authorship Analysis*. Cambridge: Cambridge University Press.

Gries, S. T. (2021). A new approach to (key) keywords analysis: Using frequency, and now also dispersion. *Research in Corpus Linguistics, 9*(2), 1–33.

Gupta, A. K., & Govindarajan, V. (2002). Cultivating a global mindset. *Academy of Management Perspectives, 16*(1), 116–26.

Heydon, G. (2019). *Researching Forensic Linguistics: Approaches and Applications*. Oxfordshire: Routledge.

Kavada, A. (2015). Social media as conversation: A manifesto. *Social Media + Society, 1*(1), 1–2.

Kilgarriff, A. (1997). Using word frequency lists to measure corpus homogeneity and similarity between corpora. In *Fifth Workshop on Very Large Corpora* (pp. 231–45). https://aclanthology.org/W97-0122.

Kiyar, M., Kubre, M. A., Collet, S. et al. (2022). Gender-affirming hormonal treatment changes neural processing of emotions in trans men: An fMRI study. *Psychoneuroendocrinology*, *146*, 105928. DOI: https://doi.org/10.1016/j.psyneuen.2022.105928.

Korenek, P., & Šimko, M. (2014). Sentiment analysis on microblog utilizing appraisal theory. *World Wide Web*, *17*(4), 847–67.

Kring, A. M., & Gordon, A. H. (1998). Sex differences in emotion: Expression, experience, and physiology. *Journal of Personality and Social Psychology*, *74*(3), 686.

Lakens, D. (2013). Calculating and reporting effect sizes to facilitate cumulative science: A practical primer for t-tests and ANOVAs. *Frontiers in Psychology*, *4*, 863.

Latu, I., Mast, M. S., & Kaiser, S. (Eds.). (2013). *Gender and Emotion: An Interdisciplinary Perspective*. Lausanne: Peter Lang AG, International Academic Publishers.

Lee, J., Lee, H. J., Song, J., & Bong, M. (2021). Enhancing children's math motivation with a joint intervention on mindset and gender stereotypes. *Learning and Instruction*, *73*, 101416.

Lehtonen, M. (2015). On sentence length distribution as an authorship attribute. In *Information Science and Applications* (pp. 811–18). Berlin, Heidelberg: Springer.

Lopez, C. (2020). *The Science Behind Good Vibrations*. https://balance.media/good-vibrations.

Martin, J. R., & White, P. R. (2005). *The Language of Evaluation* (Vol. 2). London: Palgrave Macmillan.

Martins, R., Almeida, J. J., Henriques, P., & Novais, P. (2021). A sentiment analysis approach to improve authorship identification. *Expert Systems*, *38* (5), e12469.

McMenamin, G. R. (2002). *Forensic Linguistics: Advances in Forensic Stylistics*. Boca Raton and New York: CRC Press.

Michalos, A. C. (Ed.). (2014). *Encyclopedia of Quality of Life and Well-Being Research* (Vol. 171). Dordrecht: Springer.

Narayanan, M., Gaston, J., Dozier, G. et al. (2018). Adversarial authorship, sentiment analysis, and the authorweb zoo. In *2018 IEEE Symposium Series on Computational Intelligence (SSCI)* (pp. 928–32). IEEE.

Nascimento, T., & Bianchi, M. (2021). Does TB stigma affect emotion recognition? A study with a Portuguese sample. *Does TB Stigma Affect Emotion Recognition? A Study with a Portuguese Sample*, *35*(1), 35–48.

Neogi, A. S., Garg, K. A., Mishra, R. K., & Dwivedi, Y. K. (2021). Sentiment analysis and classification of Indian farmers' protest using twitter data. *International Journal of Information Management Data Insights*, *1*(2), 100019.

Newman, M. L., Groom, C. J., Handelman, L. D., & Pennebaker, J. W. (2008). Gender differences in language use: An analysis of 14,000 text samples. *Discourse Processes, 45*(3), 211–36.

Panicheva, P., Cardiff, J., & Rosso, P. (2010). Personal sense and idiolect: Combining authorship attribution and opinion analysis. In *Proceedings of the Seventh International Conference on Language Resources and Evaluation (LREC'10)*. http://www.lrec-conf.org/proceedings/lrec2010/pdf/491_Paper.pdf.

Paschen, J. (2020). Investigating the emotional appeal of fake news using artificial intelligence and human contributions. *Journal of Product & Brand Management, 29*(2), 223–33.

Pennebaker, J. W. (2011a). *The Secret Life of Pronouns: What Our Words Say about Us*. New York: Bloomsbury Press.

Pennebaker, J. W. (2011b). Your use of pronouns reveals your personality. *Harvard Business Review, 89*(12), 32–3.

Pennebaker, J. W., & Stone, L. D. (2003). Words of wisdom: Language use over the life span. *Journal of Personality and Social Psychology, 85*(2), 291–301.

Pourdehnad, J., Warren, B., Wright, M., & Mairano, J. (2006). Unlearning/Learning Organizations: The Role of Mindset. In *Proceedings of the 50th Annual Meeting of the ISSS-2006, Sonoma, CA, USA*.

Rangel, F., Celli, F., Rosso, P., Potthast, M., Stein, B., & Daelemans. W. (2015). Overview of the 3rd Author Profiling Task at PAN 2015. In *Conference and Labs of the Evaluation Forum* (pp. 1–40).

Rangel, F., Rosso, P., Chugur, I. et al. (2014). Overview of the 2nd author profiling task at pan 2014. In *CLEF 2014 Evaluation Labs and Workshop Working Notes Papers, Sheffield, UK, 2014* (pp. 1–30).

Rayson, P., Leech, G. N., & Hodges, M. (1997). Social differentiation in the use of English vocabulary: some analyses of the conversational component of the British National Corpus. *International Journal of Corpus Linguistics, 2*(1), 133–52.

Roldos, I. (2020). 5 Sentiment Analysis Examples in Business. https://monkeylearn.com/blog/sentiment-analysis-examples.

Ruberg, W., & Steenbergh, K. (Eds.). (2011). *Sexed Sentiments: Interdisciplinary Perspectives on Gender and Emotion* (Vol. 34). Rodopi.

Rude, S., Gortner, E. M., & Pennebaker, J. (2004). Language use of depressed and depression-vulnerable college students. *Cognition & Emotion, 18*(8), 1121–33.

Ruz, G. A., Henríquez, P. A., & Mascareño, A. (2022). Bayesian constitutionalization: Twitter sentiment analysis of the Chilean constitutional process through Bayesian network classifiers. *Mathematics, 10*(2), 166.

Säily, T., Nevalainen, T., & Siirtola, H. (2011). Variation in noun and pronoun frequencies in a sociohistorical corpus of English. *Literary and Linguistic Computing, 26*(2), 167–88.

Schneider, M. (2015). *A Study on the Efficacy of Sentiment Analysis in Author Attribution.* (Doctoral dissertation, East Tennessee State University). *Electronic Theses and Dissertations.* Paper 2538. https://dc.etsu.edu/etd/2538.

Scott, M. 1998. *WordSmith Tools manual, Version 3.0.* Oxford: Oxford University Press.

Scott, M., & Tribble, C. (2006). *Textual Patterns: Key Words and Corpus Analysis in Language Education* (Vol. 22). Amsterdam and Philadelphia: John Benjamins Publishing.

Shakouri, N., Mellati, M., & Sheikhy, R. (2015). Language acquisition is hormonally-based: A plausible look. *Indian Journal of Fundamental and Applied Life Sciences, 5* (S1), 3183–9.

Sistek-Chandler, C. M. (2019). Mindset, decision making, and motivation. In *Ethical Problem-Solving and Decision-Making for Positive and Conclusive Outcomes* (pp. 37–56). IGI Global.

Solan, L. M., & Tiersma, P. M. (2004). Author identification in American courts. *Applied Linguistics, 25*(4), 448–65.

Tabachnick, B. G., & Fidell, L. S. (2007) *Using Multivariate Statistics.* New York: Pearson.

Tannen, D. (1991). *You Just Don't Understand: Women and Men in Conversation.* London: Virago.

Tausczik, Y. R., & Pennebaker, J. W. (2010). The psychological meaning of words: LIWC and computerized text analysis methods. *Journal of Language and Social Psychology, 29*(1), 24–54.

Taylor, C. (2013). Searching for similarity using corpus-assisted discourse studies. *Corpora, 8*(1), 81–113.

Taylor, C., & Marchi, A. (2018). *Corpus Approaches to Discourse. A Critical Review.* New York: Routledge.

Torney, R., Vamplew, P., & Yearwood, J. (2012). Using psycholinguistic features for profiling first language of authors. *Journal of the American Society for Information Science and Technology, 63*(6), 1256–1269.

Townsend, L., & Wallace, C. (2016). Social media research: A guide to ethics. Economic and Social Research Council [grant number ES/M001628/1]. University of Aberdeen. https://aofirs.org/research-papers/social-media/social-media-research-a-guide-to-ethics.

Verplanken, B., & Orbell, S. (2019). Habit and behaviour change. *Social Psychology in Action: Evidence-Based Interventions from Theory to Practice*, 65–78.

Wiegmann, M., Stein, B., & Potthast, M. (2019). Overview of the celebrity profiling task at PAN 2019. In *Conference and Labs of the Evaluation Forum (Working Notes)*. https://pan.webis.de/downloads/publications/papers/wiegmann_2019.pdf.

Zang, C., Fu, Y., Bai, X., Yan, G., & Liversedge, S. P. (2018). Investigating word length effects in Chinese reading. *Journal of Experimental Psychology: Human Perception and Performance, 44*(12), 1831–41.

Zangerle, E., Mayerl, M., Specht, G., Potthast, M., & Stein, B. (2020). Overview of the style change detection task at PAN 2020. In *Conference and Labs of the Evaluation Forum (Working Notes)*. https://ceur-ws.org/Vol-2696/paper_256.pdf.

Zhang, B. (2022) *Dictionary of Modern Chinese Function Words* (6th ed.). Beijing: The Commercial Press.

Zhang, S. (2016). Authorship attribution and feature testing for short Chinese emails. *International Journal of Speech, Language & the Law, 23*(1). https://journals.equinoxpub.com/OLDIJSLL/article/view/20300/27542.

Zhang, S. (2019). From keywords to authorship profiling: A keyness approach. Unpublished research proposal.

Zhang, S. (2021). From flaming to incited crime: Recognising cyberbullying on Chinese wechat account. *International Journal for the Semiotics of Law-Revue internationale de Sémiotique juridique, 34*(4), 1093–116.

Zhang, W. (2004) *SPSS Advanced Statistics*. Beijing: Higher Education Press.

Zhou, Y. (2007). Words that Matter: Gender Features in the Language Use of Weblog. Unpublished master's dissertation. Zhejiang University.

Acknowledgements

I am profoundly grateful to a host of individuals whose support and contributions have been invaluable throughout this journey. Firstly, my deepest gratitude goes to Tim Grant, whose continuous support and assistance were the cornerstone that made this work possible. I also extend my sincere thanks to Tammy Gales for providing me the precious opportunity to conduct this study, which is an experience that has been immensely educational and rewarding.

Special appreciation is extended to the editorial staff, Ankita Dutta and Julia, for their warm reminders and diligence that greatly assisted the publication process. I am particularly indebted to Terry Royce, whose patience and insightful suggestions during the proofreading stage significantly enhanced the quality of my work. My thanks also go to Richard Yuan for his valuable suggestions, which have been greatly beneficial.

I express my heartfelt gratitude to Prof. Du Jinbang for his unwavering encouragement, which has been a source of strength throughout this endeavour. My sincere appreciation also extends to the anonymous reviewers. Their discerning perspectives and constructive feedback were instrumental in the essential refining of my work.

On a personal note, I reserve my big thanks for my family. To my husband, Ge Fei, your constant support has been my pillar of strength. Your faith in me has rendered this journey enjoyable.

I also wish to acknowledge all the authors, who are willing to share their writings and students, especially Lin Lin, Chen Shuyan, and Ye Tongyin. Their contributions to data collection and other related tasks have been immense and deeply appreciated.

Lastly, completing this work has been a challenging but rewarding journey, made possible by the collective effort and goodwill of each individual mentioned here, along with many others who have offered their support in various ways. To one and all, I am eternally grateful.

Responsibility for any remaining errors rests solely with the author.

This study is supported by the National Social Science Project of China (Project No.: 20BYY073).

Cambridge Elements ⁼

Forensic Linguistics

Tim is one of the world's most experienced forensic linguistic practitioners and his case work has involved the analysis of abusive and threatening communications in many different contexts including investigations into sexual assault, stalking, murder, and terrorism. He also makes regular media contributions including presenting police appeals such as for the BBC Crimewatch programme.

Tammy Gales
Hofstra University

Tammy Gales is an Associate Professor of Linguistics and the Director of Research at the Institute for Forensic Linguistics, Threat Assessment, and Strategic Analysis at Hofstra University, New York. She has served on the Executive Committee for the International Association of Forensic Linguists (IAFL), is on the editorial board for the peer-reviewed journals Applied Corpus Linguistics and Language and Law / Linguagem e Direito, and is a member of the advisory board for the BYU Law and Corpus Linguistics group. Her research interests cross the boundaries of forensic linguistics and language and the law, with a primary focus on threatening communications. She has trained law enforcement agents from agencies across Canada and the U.S. and has applied her work to both criminal and civil cases.

About the Series

Elements in Forensic Linguistics provides high-quality accessible writing, bringing cutting-edge forensic linguistics to students and researchers as well as to practitioners in law enforcement and law. Elements in the series range from descriptive linguistics work, documenting a full range of legal and forensic texts and contexts; empirical findings and methodological developments to enhance research, investigative advice, and evidence for courts; and explorations into the theoretical and ethical foundations of research and practice in forensic linguistics.

Cambridge Elements ☰

Forensic Linguistics

Elements in the Series

The Idea of Progress in Forensic Authorship Analysis
Tim Grant

Forensic Linguistics in the Philippines: Origins, Developments, and Directions
Marilu Rañosa-Madrunio and Isabel Pefianco Martin

The Language of Fake News
Jack Grieve and Helena Woodfield

A Theory of Linguistic Individuality for Authorship Analysis
Andrea Nini

Forensic Linguistics in Australia: Origins, Progress and Prospects
Diana Eades, Helen Fraser, and Georgina Heydon

Online Child Sexual Grooming Discourse
Nuria Lorenzo-Dus, Craig Evans, and Ruth Mullineux-Morgan

Spoken Threats from Production to Perception
James Tompkinson

The Language of Romance Crimes: Interactions of Love, Money, and Threat
Elisabeth Carter

Authorship Analysis in Chinese Social Media Texts
Shaomin Zhang

A full series listing is available at: www.cambridge.org/EIFL

Printed in the United States
by Baker & Taylor Publisher Services